Wendy and Lucy

Photo: Penny Dudley

Wendy Dudley, an Ontario-born writer, artist, and media consultant, has called Alberta home since 1977. Bestowed with an avid curiosity about life, she spent 15 years as a reporter with the *Calgary Herald*, covering Native affairs, country music, rural issues, and western heritage.

Wendy now works from her home in the Alberta foothills, where she lives with her mother, a mule, two donkeys, two dogs, and a varying number of barn cats. She has written and narrated stories about her life in the high country for cbc Radio; her writing also appears in several publications, including the *Western Producer, Alberta Crops and Beef, AlbertaViews, Legacy,* and *EnviroLine.* Practising what she preaches, Wendy believes that people should enjoy life, that peaceful retreats are as much cerebral as they are physical, and that everyone has a homeplace—they just need to discover where it is.

For my mother and father, who broke trail

don't name the ducks

and other truths
about life in the country

To Rietta
Enjoy hiking this trail of tales!
Wendy

Wendy Dudley

2020

FIFTH
HOUSE

Cover and interior design by Articulate Eye
Interior illustrations by Wendy Dudley
Cover photograph Andrew Wenzel / Masterfile
Cover background photograph David Berezowski / Great Bear Enterprises
Edited/copyedited by Alex Rettie; proofread by Ann Sullivan
Scans by St. Solo Computer Graphics

While all of the events in this book are true, some of the names of people have been changed to protect their privacy.

The publisher gratefully acknowledges the support of The Canada Council for the Arts and the Department of Canadian Heritage.

Canada Council   Conseil des Arts
for the Arts   du Canada

We acknowledge the financial support of the Government of Canada through the Book Publishing Industry Development Program (BPIDP) for our publishing activities.

Printed in Canada by Friesens

04 05 06 07 / 5 4 3 2

National Library of Canada Cataloguing in Publication Data

Dudley, Wendy, 1955-
   Don't name the ducks, and other truths about life in the high country / by Wendy Dudley.

   ISBN 1-894856-28-7

   1. Dudley, Wendy, 1955- —Anecdotes. 2. Country life—Alberta—Bow River Region—Anecdotes. 3. Bow River Region (Alta.)—Anecdotes. I. Title.

FC3695.B67Z49 2003   971.23'3   C2003-910439-7
F1079.B67D82 2003

Fifth House Ltd.   In the United States:
A Fitzhenry & Whiteside Company   Fitzhenry & Whiteside
1511, 1800-4 St. SW   121 Harvard Avenue, Suite 2
Calgary, Alberta T2S 2S5   Allston, MA 02134
1-800-387-9776
www.fitzhenry.ca

Contents

Foreword

The countryside flowed beneath our tires. A snow-covered road is quieter than pavement, and we had the feeling we were gliding over the swells of a wide, frozen sea. This was the rangeland of southwest Alberta: land caught between the mountains and the plains in a comfortable blend of rolling hills and wooded valleys. A skiff of snow described natural topographic patterns and highlighted weathered barns, sheds, and fences that fitted the landscape like a well-worn saddle. It was an Andrew Wyeth world with a cowboy twist. Because of this I was wearing a grin. My eyes were shooting possible painting compositions I would never have time to do. They were also scanning every fence post and every aspen for my "jinx" bird, the great grey owl—I have never seen one in the wild. However, I knew that this was great grey country because Wendy had told me that she had seen them many times near her home in Burro Alley.

This was my first time visiting Wendy and her mother, Penny, at Burro Alley. Wendy has always been an "aw-shucks," self-deprecating kind of girl, and though I was expecting a pleasant homestead, I did not expect it to be so perfectly to my taste. The snow, aspen, and spruce, along with the smaller buildings and the house, were arranged in pleasing compositions as we drove down the lane and walked from the car to the front door. Inside we were greeted with warmth and comfort for the eye, from the honey-coloured log walls, to the rugs and cozy furniture.

And there were Wendy and Penny. Wendy, of course, has changed since I first knew her as a young child, but Penny seemed to be the same slender, vivacious, no-nonsense woman I first met in the late 1940s. Penny and her husband, Ken, were part of the heart of our folksong group that gathered first in 1947, and still meets to this day. We would play guitars and sing the old campfire standards of Burl Ives, cowboy songs, spirituals, English and Scottish ballads, and so on. Ken was always expected to do a yodelling number, especially "My Old Canadian Home." Now, half a century later, I was standing in the Dudleys' "old Canadian home." It was perfect.

This book is the story of Burro Alley and its living things. Wendy weaves stories about nature with stories of the cattlemen and cowboys and their culture. One of my favourite chapters concerns Ian Tyson and the community of Longview, Alberta. Tyson's ballads tell of a vanishing way of life. There was a heart and soul in that life that is missing in the new, mechanized world of agribusiness. Wendy adds her stories to Ian's. Without sentimentality or lamentation, she does honour to a rich part of our human heritage, which is still clinging to existence in the buffeting arena of 21st century economics and industrialization. Her phrase "the rural, handmade life" is just right. *Don't Name the Ducks* is the saga of a very individual, rural, handmade life.

From the young girl visiting our home on the Niagara Escarpment, to the young woman showing us the osprey's nest, to the professional journalist asking me penetrating questions, I know that Wendy is a unique human being. Although I can't exactly explain what is meant by a "big heart," Wendy's qualifies. Her deep feelings for our natural and human heritage go far beyond the philosophical; they are intense and personal. And Wendy knows that, just as each human fingerprint in history is unique and each zebra pattern has never been repeated, each living thing is an individual. That is why she must name her ducks.

Individuality, respect, and love—these things matter and are what this book is about.

This is also a book of adventures, accidents, and mishaps, ranging from skunks to leafy spurge. Wendy makes clear what I have always known to be one of her characteristics: in the face of adversity, a laugh helps to lighten the load. Wendy's sense of humour has her chuckling about herself quite regularly. She doesn't chuckle about sour gas wells, however. She has the toughness of a good journalist and the conscience of an ardent environmentalist. I know that she could write another book about what modern man is doing to this planet. We see eye to eye on that score.

Wendy's own drawings fit very well with the mood of the book. They are accurate but they go well beyond to portray the warmth and particularity that is so much a part of her being.

As you enter this book you will have the same feeling I had when I entered Wendy's log home. It will envelop you in its warmth. To repeat her phrase used in another sense, through her writing she "has left a welcome footprint in cow country."

I did not see my great grey owl, but Wendy showed me the post where one had perched not long before. I'll just have to go back, but in the meantime, this book will take me there. It is a worthwhile visit for everyone.

Robert Bateman
Salt Spring Island, BC
2003

Acknowledgements

There are many people who share the journey of writing a book. Without them, it would be an arduous trek; with them, it is an exciting adventure. I would like to pass along my thanks to my parents, Ken and Penny—without them, who would I be?; to my brother, Jon, for sharing those early paths; to my dear friend, novelist Rick Mofina, for being there, always; to writer Marsha Boulton, for her everlasting faith; to authors Brian Brennan and Bruce Masterman, for their unselfish support; to the late Timothy Findley, W. O. Mitchell, and Grant McEwan—their creativity and passion for the natural world inspired me deeply; to Susan Scott, for taking a chance those many years ago; to the late Ken Hull, who took that chance and ran with it; to Mike Spear and Bev Oberg at CBC Radio, who laughed and cheered in all the right spots; to the staff at Fifth House, for sharing and understanding my vision; to all the animals that have enriched my life, for without them, there would be no Burro Alley; and to all those who work to protect ranchland and wilderness places.

Introduction

This is a story about coming home to what matters.

As a child, I built forts in the tangled sumac bush above the sand and clay bluffs overlooking Lake Ontario. My family lived on the edge of a ravine, our backyard reaching into the wilds, where there were fox, raccoons, deer, and pheasants. Most days after school, I hiked the gully trails, always with our dog at my side, flushing rabbits from the underbrush while listening to the cries of seagulls and terns flying over the lake. At the back of our home was a rustic log cabin where I spent hours painting portraits of moose, whisky-jacks, and Tom Thomson-inspired images of storms brewing over white-capped lakes. I was fascinated by the outdoors and its many creatures, amusing our neighbours with a pet skunk and young hawk. I even tried keeping a toad until one evening I lifted him from his glass terrarium, plopping him down on our front lawn in the shade of a sprawling elm. Just for a few minutes, I thought, so he can enjoy a bit of freedom. Two hours later, I remembered he was still loose. Everyone joined in the search, illuminating our lawn with probing flashlights. But my warty friend had hopped away to a new home, a better one I am sure, beneath some damp moss and brown leaves. And then there was Travis, a baby black squirrel, so deformed he had to tilt his head sideways to eat while teetering on a shrivelled, undeveloped, foot. Perched on my shoulder, he would share a turkey drumstick with me, sometimes grabbing it and scampering off to finish his feast under my bed.

I also made friends with his cousins, the white-bellied red squirrels that chattered away in the northern bush, where we had a cabin just outside Algonquin Park. There, my brother and I built tree houses, tapped the maple trees, skated on the lake, and canoed among beaver lodges. In the evenings, we sat around the wood stove, reading such books as Ernest Thompson Seton's *Wild Animals I Have Known*, Jack London's *Call of the Wild*, the poems of Robert Service, and Mary O'Hara's *My Friend Flicka*.

Sometimes my dad would strum his old guitar, entertaining us with cowboy songs he learned while breaking horses on the Circle M Ranch, a dude ranch and Western movie lot north of Toronto. I probably got my first inklings about moving west from reading my dad's hardcover collection of Will James books: *Smoky, Sand, Cow Country, Lone Cowboy,* and *All in a Day's Riding.* What a wonderful way to lope the West without ever putting a toe in the stirrup, but what strange looks I received when I stood before my Grade 8 classmates, giving a report on James's book *Cowboy in the Making.* There were more frowns when I clip-clopped down my high-school hallways wearing scruffy cowboy boots. It was obvious my friends and I did not wander the same trails.

When I left home, travelling across Canada and the United States on a Greyhound bus, I took my memories with me. I was searching for a new home, one where I could fly on my own. Awed by the giant firs on the West Coast and by the killer whales swimming the inside passages, I spent several years in Vancouver, beachcombing, cycling oceanside paths, and hiking lush green trails. One autumn after several years, I migrated inland to Banff, where I climbed mountain passes and rafted whitewater rivers. I eventually moved to Calgary, where I decided to put down roots. With the mountains shadowing the western horizon and the prairies and sloughs stretching to the east, this fringe on the plains appealed to me. Here was an abundance of goat trails and a labyrinth of wild rivers and blue lakes, miles of open grasslands, and endless fields bucking with Will James's horses. And holding it all together was a big, magnificent sky.

For several years, I lived in a tiny home along the Bow River in Calgary, where I whiled away evenings perched on a rock with my orange cat Tod. Pretending to fish, we would watch minute water creatures swirl in the back eddies while waving to the common mergansers that sailed by. I knew where the fox hunted, where the beaver lived, and where the bald eagles perched. Always, the land was calling; I needed to find a home outside the city.

Home can be a tired farm, an extravagant castle, a lakeside shack, or a downtown apartment; it is where you feel comfortable. For me, home is where the sky reflects a horizon, where there is room to think. I hunger for wild sounds and smells. The soil I dug in as a child is still stuck between my toes. I am rooted to land, possessed by it.

When I moved to the foothills, it was like a homecoming. Once again, I could see the stars at night, smell the earth in spring, and hear the creek sing in the morning. Here I can croak with the ravens, yodel with the coyotes, and whistle with the elk. Once again, dogs hike at my side.

When my mother moved in, the circle was complete. When the horse, mule, and donkeys moved in, it was like having my dad back in the saddle. Our log house became our homeplace, that special place full of memories, a place that travels with you forever as a companion.

This is the story of that place. We call it Burro Alley Ranch, in honour of the longears that make us smile most every day.

Chapter One

Lame Excuse

With my right leg dangling like a limp fishing line and my face smeared with dirt and sweat, I stood there like a naughty child caught playing hooky from school. My mother's voice was stern, her words stinging as much as the pain now gripping my groin.

"Why do you ride that animal without a saddle? And why don't you put a bit in her?"

"She didn't do anything wrong!" I screamed back, defending my long-eared friend as I clutched my leg. But my argument was lost on the wind. Seconds later, I crumpled to the ground, my groin cramping in spasms from the knifelike pain creeping down my inside right thigh.

Only moments before, I had been riding my mule Lucy bareback, using her rope halter and lead as a bitless bridle while rounding up the donkeys to bring them back to the barn for the night. The roundup was a lazy summer afternoon ritual. Leaving the house with the halter and lead draped over my shoulder, I would stroll the fields, never knowing exactly where I would find my animals grazing. Maybe in an open pocket or maybe in the bush playing hide-and-seek, their dark coats and the black aspen trunks becoming one. Once I found Lucy, I would slip on her halter, then lead her to a log or higher ground where I could easily swing my leg over her broad back. She always stood still, knowing I would give a gentle squeeze

Riding bareback is a wonderful way to develop balance, the rhythm of your hips matching the cadence of hoof beats.

with my legs when we were ready to move on. With the two donkeys trotting in front like obedient pups, Lucy and I worked as a team, my leg cues guiding her around the trees and through the bush. She wore no bit, and there were no reins to hang onto, just a small hank of mane, its spiky hair as short as a cropped pasture.

I was proud of Lucy. Sure, she could be a knothead at times, but that's when her nostrils detected the musky smell of bear or cougar. Rather than being stubborn, she possessed a keen sense of self-preservation, always on alert when dark shadows fluttered among the aspen bluffs or spruce groves. But today there was a mischievous wind tugging at the long grasses, and the warmth of the spring sun spirited my small herd into frivolous play. The two donkeys darted out front, their swinging heads and merry kicks inviting Lucy to join their cheeky trot.

I didn't try to hold her back. "Sure, let's go down the hill," I said. "Then we'll circle around and head back home." I'm not sure what happened next, but I imagine I began sliding towards her neck. Lucy doesn't have withers, so it's easy to creep over her shoulders when riding downhill. I do remember gripping with my legs, determined to stay on her back as my arms embraced her thick neck.

I hit the ground hard, hip first and then a somersault. Colliding with a rock poking out of the clay-hard ground, I felt a burst of pain crack like a stitch of lightning. For several minutes, I lay there, trying to catch my breath, wondering what went wrong. Lucy hadn't bolted, spooked, bucked, or reared. In fact, she was now standing next to me, while the two donkeys raced around the field braying their high-pitched alarm. Then they too trotted over, drooping their shaggy heads over my shoulder. When I whimpered in pain, they resumed their anxious race, braying until the narrow valley vibrated with their screams.

With every muscle, ligament, and tendon in my groin on fire, I began dragging myself up the hill, eyeing a stand of aspen trees at the top. I used my elbows to pull my body along, the injured leg dragging behind as if it was no longer attached to the rest of me. Grimacing, I thought of all those cowboys who have broken bones on the job. What would they do? What would Will James do? Find a tree and fashion a branch into a crutch so he could hobble his way home. Pulling myself up the rough trunk of a tree, I broke off a low limb. It was no use—my leg was now in a spasm, a mere toe-touch to the ground sending me to the stars. The half-mile back to the house seemed like ten miles. I could feel the warm wind turning cold as it shifted from the west to the north. I began to shiver.

Having heard the piercing donkey brays, Mom suspected something was wrong. When she crested the hill, she saw me standing there with my hand on my leg and a gnarled branch in my hand.

"Now what have you done?" she yelled.

I explained my sorry state.

"Why do you do such stupid things? Next time, try using a saddle," she shouted, her words as biting as the icy wind. "Just sit there, while I take the animals back. And then I guess I'll try driving the car along the road to get you." I stared at my mother in disbelief. At age seventy-seven, she hasn't driven a day in her life. "Don't be crazy," I yelled back. "You don't have a licence. You'll never make it this far. You'll end up in an accident, and then we'll be in a real mess."

"Fine," she grumbled. "I'll take the animals back and call an ambulance."

I leaned back in the grass, watching her take Lucy by the lead, pulling her hard when she firmly planted all four hooves and refused to budge. I wanted to yell out to Mom that she shouldn't pull with constant pressure, that she should give separate tugs or else Lucy would brace her body, making it impossible to win the battle. But I kept quiet. Lying there on my backside and considering my unceremonious crash to the ground, I didn't think it wise to offer peanut-gallery advice.

"Are you OK?" came a whispered voice from the side of the road. Stretched out, with my hands over my face, I guess I didn't look like I was taking an afternoon nap. I propped myself up and answered, "Well, actually, no, I'm not." The girl came to my side with her father, a nearby neighbour.

"My dad was driving by, and he thought you were a dead animal," she said. I smiled at her honesty. "Well, he wasn't far from the truth," I replied. "I do sort of feel like a carcass. I'm just glad your dad didn't come back with his gun."

My neighbours stayed with me until the ambulance arrived, the little girl's conversation keeping my spirits high. When the paramedics attempted to move me onto the stretcher, I rolled my shoulders, thinking I could at least give them a hand moving my more than featherweight body, but a sharp verbal bark pushed me back.

"Look," one paramedic said. "I think you've broken your hip. And you've got a femoral artery sitting right there that you don't want to sever." My world went dark, my face pale. I tried to hold the tears back as I felt the weight of his words. I was in serious trouble. It took two paramedics and two firefighters to haul me uphill and over a barbed wire fence to where the ambulance was waiting. Twenty-four hours later I was in surgery. Three pins were screwed into the neck of my upper femur. I heard more times than necessary how serious an injury it was, how I was at risk for blood clots, and how, even with the operation, the hip could still die. The morphine numbed the physical pain, carrying me into a desert full of spotted horses with pounding hoofs; but the drug could not kill the reality of what lay ahead.

At least three months on crutches before I could put any weight on my leg. No working, no driving, no bending. No nothing.

I thought of this year's hay that I wouldn't be cutting, drying, or stacking. I thought of mom slaving with the daily chores. I thought of the tree stretched across the back fence, the broken strands of wire loose on the ground. I thought of my mule and donkeys growing fat with no exercise. I thought of myself growing fatter with no exercise. I thought of my dogs, Maggie and Georgie, and how I would miss walking them to the creek for their daily swim. I thought of my blind cat Hud and how he would be the only living creature that wouldn't notice anything different about me.

My wallow in self-pity was abruptly interrupted when my surgeon arrived at the end of my bed with several interns. "Now here's a young lady who fractured her femur when she fell off her . . . " He paused, then added with confidence, "fell off her mule."

"You receive full marks for that," I smiled. "I can't believe you remembered to call her a mule and not a horse."

Over the next two days, I contemplated how I would spend my three months of convalescence. "You're going to go insane," a neighbour warned. "In two weeks, when you're feeling better, the only thing holding you back will be that leg. And you're going to get real cranky."

A project, I thought. I need to find a project. And then it hit me. It was time to write a book, something I'd put off for two years because there never seemed enough time. I no longer had that excuse.

I would write about life in the country and my adventures on Burro Alley Ranch. I would write about my herding dog that's terrified of sheep, about the hard-headed grouse that crash through our windows, a duck that took an ice bath, and a bear that tried to steal a bag of bananas. And, of course, I would write about my posse of mule and donkeys.

And so, for several minutes, I forgot about my leg and began to think about tomorrow.

Chapter Two

Wild Beginnings

I was only nine years old, but I will never forget the summer I discovered Grey Owl and his beavers.

My admiration for this conservation crusader grew with every page of his autobiographical *Pilgrims of the Wild*. My tears tumbled like a creek in spring flood when I reached the part where his pet beavers McGinnis and McGinty disappear forever, their mournful wailings only a memory. Never again would they chortle over sweet candies, never again would they gambol like children; they were gone, most likely killed by a trapper but perhaps, Grey Owl and I hoped, only lost to the wilderness in which they were intended to live. Wrenched by such emotional passages, I would abandon the book on a mossy tree stump and stumble off in search of my dog. Listening to every word of this tragic story, she put the world right by slurping away my salty tears.

Over the next few years, I read most of Grey Owl's books during the summer and winter vacations we spent on Lucy Lake, a gentle beaver pond cradled in the rounded hills near Ontario's Algonquin Park, a marvellous quilt of granite cliffs, dark waters, moose bogs, and maple forests. Here, where animal trails were more common than roadways, it was easy to become part of Grey Owl's wilderness. I walked summer bushland trails in moccasins and packed winter paths on rawhide snowshoes, living my

During winter blizzards, wolves would move across our lake, hiding behind a curtain of snow, their heads down, their eyes slanted.

own version of stories told in *Tales of an Empty Cabin* and *Men of the Last Frontier.*

My father built our cabin on Lucy's shores when I was three, and it became my childhood home on weekends and school holidays. Our heat radiated from a coal-black wood stove, its fuel chopped and stacked by hand. Our amber light came from oil lamps; our water was hauled from the lake in metal buckets, the chopping of the winter water hole a regular morning chore. In spring we tapped the trees with wooden spiles, boiling the sap into sweet and sticky maple syrup in fire-blackened washtubs. In summer we swam among the lily pads, seeing if we could get close enough to the loons to see their red eyes. In winter we watched a pageant of northern lights while skating on a rink lit by storm lanterns. The night always took on an exciting chill when the wolves moved across the frozen lake, their chorus of howls raising the hackles of our soft-bellied lapdogs.

During autumn evenings, when the sky's blue spilled into a deep wine red, I often watched a pair of beaver swim across a secluded bay, their plump dark bodies surfacing at the marshy shoreline. Together, they would waddle towards a stand of birch, preparing for their nocturnal chew. Thinking of Grey Owl and how he once made his living as a fur trapper, I worried about the beavers' future, fearing they would die a cruel death when the local trapper arrived with his battery of traps.

Skirting the lake's icebound shores, I combed the terrain for the ghastly steel fangs. Some were tucked beneath logs, where I would discover red squirrels, their tiny bodies cold and stiff, crushed by massive jaws intended for larger animals. But sometimes I arrived in time, spotting a chain attached to a pole embedded in the frozen beaver dam. Tracing its links below the lake's dark surface, I would probe the mud with a thick stick, jumping back when the trap suddenly snapped shut and split my maple pole as if it were a brittle bone.

I would flee in tears, convinced the trapper would track me down and demand payment for the loss of a pelt. Maybe he would throw my parents behind bars, declaring it bushland justice. Or, I hoped, he would curse the sprung trap, believing he'd been outsmarted by the beaver. Yes, that was it! I would tell him I didn't know anything about his trap, that the beaver must have cleverly sprung it by teasing it with a stick.

I don't remember how my parents reacted to my tearful confession, but I do know I was not severely reprimanded. After all, it would be difficult to punish me for sharing their belief that all animals—from the deer mice and flying squirrels that visited our bird feeders at night to the lumbering moose and brown-muzzled bears that shared our walking trails—were precious and worth saving from a gruesome death.

Wild animals were always welcome at our camp, up to a point, that is. I can still see that corn broom swinging through the air, my mother swatting at a hefty bruin bent on coming through our screen door to snatch a still-warm wild raspberry pie off the kitchen table. Our other wild guests included deer, mink, otters, and, of course, grey jays, the proverbial camp robbers we called whisky-jacks. We'd be gone from the cabin for months, but within minutes of our arrival the jays would swoop in, as if the smoke curls from our chimney had signalled the arrival of Those Who Bring Gifts of Sunflower Seeds.

I was indeed my parents' child, rooted in nature from my first breath. Mom used to say I was practically born in a canoe. My parents worked summers in Algonquin Park, where the Group of Seven so gloriously captured on canvas the area's wild northern spirit and vivid fall colours. My dad taught canoeing, while Mom cooked for construction camps—until some of the men thought it funny to chop off the chipmunks' tails and pin them to their hats. She quit in disgust.

Living in a wedge tent on Canoe Lake, Mom befriended a moose, a long-legged beauty she named Evelyn. Every day at the same time, Evelyn crashed through the underbrush, heading down to the lake for her afternoon drink. However, her route was a little too close to mom's firepit. It wasn't that mom feared the clumsy animal; she just wasn't fussy about having Evelyn sample the pies she was cooking over the fire's embers. Instead, mom offered her bread, and the two became best of friends. With Evelyn now eating from Mom's hands, she was close enough to reveal her true gender. Evelyn underwent a name change; she was now known as Bruce the Moose.

Mom learned about wilderness survival from Dad, who was raised in Toronto when the Don Valley Parkway was still a wooded riverway. He and his mother would camp in the valley, living in their homemade tepees. My dad consumed every survival skill taught between the covers of Ernest Thompson Seton's *Two Little Savages*, and he continued to praise the book's lessons long after my brother and I were born. Dad was a holdover from the pioneer days. He was breaking horses on a ranch near Kleinberg, north of Toronto, when he met my mother. When they married in 1943, Mom also wedded a life devoted to the natural world.

During their years in Algonquin Park, Mom met another wonderful teacher, Bea Baskerville, a widowed woodswoman whom I met years later when we stayed at our own cabin near the park. Bea had a way with wild animals, and I can still see the raccoons she invited into her kitchen for evening snacks. She always knew when they were there, having trained them to ring an outside bell to announce their arrival. Bea died many years ago, but her spirit lives on in her hooked rug of artist Tom Thomson's *The Jack Pine*, a family treasure we hang above the fireplace.

My dad has since died of cancer, but he left me his love of wilderness literature and his campfire stories about fishing trips with Lorne Greene, the CBC Radio broadcaster who later made his fortune as Pa Cartwright on the *Bonanza* TV series. We gave my dad a creekside memorial service in Alberta's Rocky Mountains, a region he loved to hike. Launching him on his final journey, we flung his ashes into a swift-moving river. That special spot remains private, but it's a place where the country still smells wild and where Dad can dream of moonlight shining silver on Lucy Lake.

.   .   .

That trapper never did come to our door, and I continued to ferret out his traps, believing no animal should have to chew off its leg and struggle on three limbs, or drown on a lake bottom with its paw clenched in a trap. Lucy Lake is now just a fond memory, but my days there seeded my reverence for the natural world. When I discovered Grey Owl those many years ago, he became a kindred spirit. I was a loner, but through his words I found someone who shared and understood my passion for wildlife. It didn't matter to me that Grey Owl wasn't really an Indian, his deception revealed after his death. What did matter was the message he delivered to the world, one which sought respect for the creatures we live with and the land and waters we share with them. A conservationist before his time, he spoke of stewardship instead of superiority.

I didn't know it then, but my youth at Lucy Lake— may its waters always carry a forging V of beavers—and the writings of Grey Owl would stay with me for years to come, following me from the Ontario bushland to the spruce and aspen foothills of the Rocky Mountains, where the air quakes with drumming grouse and where I walk trails worn smooth by coyotes, grizzlies, cougars, and lynx. Where I now live, a creek gurgles outside my window; its lush banks shade a trampled path. The beaver live here too.

Chapter Three

Of Cows and Girls

I fell in love with all things barnyard during my first high-school summer job, when I worked on a dairy farm near Lindsay, in cow country northeast of Toronto. It was two months of glorious back-breaking labour, a summer that sent me home with calloused hands, bulging biceps, and a determination to one day own my own piece of rural heaven.

Part of a provincial agriculture program, the student job was supposed to teach urban teenagers like me about the source of our food. Now, I had a pretty good idea that my milk came from a cow, that my eggs came from chickens, and that pork came from a pig, but I didn't have a clue about how the food got from the gate to the plate. When I filled out the application, I was hoping for a summer of sunshine and fun.

How thrilled I was to be picked, along with a dozen or so other students, for this pilot project. With a whopping salary of seven dollars a day, at six days a week, I had hit the jackpot! If I was dancing on clouds, my host farmer, Bill, was kicking the dirt. He wanted a strapping young lad, not a tender-footed girl! He sized me up pretty quick, all five feet of me. So this is what they sent me to help milk my barn of cows, bale my township of hay, and stack my acres of mow? To make matters worse, I didn't even know how to drive, never mind plough a field. And it didn't help that Bill's farm

On hot afternoons, I would sit on the farm porch, shelling pea pods, and on warm nights I would sleep there, inhaling the perfume of cows and sweet hay.

was already filled with females—three young daughters all under twelve years old.

"Well, I don't know what I should have you do," Bill said over breakfast on my first morning, his brow furrowed with self-pity. "Clean out the calf pen, I guess. See what kind of job you can do with that."

An hour later, I was standing knee-high in soiled straw. Oh boy, my first stall to muck out! Wearing brand-new, stiff leather gloves and a crisp new work shirt, I dug into my chore like a hungry man digging into a mound of buttery, hot mashed potatoes. I was having fun all right, but gee, this job seemed to be taking hours. For every fork of manure I picked up, half slipped through the tines. But I persisted, determined to show Bill I was up to the job, that I was made of the right stuff. He'd see, I could do twice the job of that brawny high-school football player he'd hoped for.

When noon rolled around, Bill came looking for me. He chatted a bit, then casually folded his arms. I was sure I detected a smile skipping across his ruddy face. "You've done a real good job," he said. "But next time, it might be easier if you use the manure fork instead of the hay fork."

Bill was a great teacher but an unforgiving boss, so I made sure I never complained. Not when he had me heave hay bales without gloves, the twine digging into my fingers, the blisters bursting before we left the first field. And not when he made me pay for the roadside mailbox I sheered off with the tractor. Besides, I adored this farm, with its doe-eyed Jersey cows, its smell of early morning dew, and its shed full of cranky tractors. It would be eighteen more years before I received my driver's licence, but by summer's end I had graduated from a gentle grey Ford tractor to a multi-geared fire-engine-red International Harvester.

And I soon got over my shyness about calling in the

cows for their morning milking. At first, I worried about waking the neighbours with all that hooting, but it wasn't long before I had them marching in single file under my command. In the beginning, they played bovine jokes, cramming into each other's milking stalls and gazing at me as if they'd lost their way. And then Bill would arrive, looking like a Jack Russell terrier on the hunt. "What's that one doing over there?" he'd snap. "She's supposed to be over here, in the next row."

I'd shrug my shoulders and bow my head, taking full blame for not knowing one fawn-coloured Jersey from another. Eventually, the bossies and I worked it out, and I learned which ones had sensitive udders and which ones would sooner slap your face with their whiplike tails than learn the meaning of patience.

I'm not at my best in the morning, but that was one summer I didn't mind tumbling out of bed before 6 AM. The barn cats would gather beneath the cows, waiting for a frothy squirt, and on cool mornings I too delighted in a taste of warm, creamy milk, fresh from Mamma cow's udder.

A day in the mow, however, was like a day pouring hot tar. Above the barn's stalls, the hay attic was a blazing cauldron, the air a thick stew of heat and dust. As the bales tumbled off the conveyer, I wrestled them into orderly stacks. The pace was fast and unforgiving. If I didn't stack the bales tightly, my leg would plunge into the deep and dark gaps, jolting my knee and hip as if I'd stepped into a badger hole. Miss a beat, and the bales landed every which way, bouncing off each other in a haphazard free-for-all. But it was my work in the mow that promoted me from a mere city girl to a genuine hired hand.

It was a particularly hot afternoon when Bill's father offered to work the mow. "No," Bill answered, without

giving it further thought. "I want her up there. She's good."
With that boost of confidence, I threw the bales higher
and faster. I found a rhythm, tossing them in a single fluid
motion, from the ground to my thighs to the top of the
stack. The sky was my limit. I thought of the Women's Land
Army, those 80,000 British city women who flocked to the
fields during the Second World War. They felled trees, ran
threshing gangs, and tended to livestock, feeding a nation. I
would not let them down!

So what if several days later I drove the tractor into the
rear end of the combine, crumpling the bale chute like an
accordion and pushing the machine out the other side of the
barn? Darn tractor, the brakes were soft. Or the clutch was
acting up. Or something.

And so what if I embarrassed Bill when I sobbed over a
sick cow? Men cry too, you know. One of his best milkers lay
crumpled in the back field, her eyes dull and her breathing
slow. She had hardware disease, a serious inflammation of
the bovine stomach. Cows often swallow without chewing,
leaving them vulnerable to ingesting bits of wire, staples, or
nails. The metal lodges in their stomach, which before long
becomes infected. In great pain, the cow finds it hard to
walk, and eventually she stops eating. If left untreated, she
usually dies. Some farmers insert magnets into their cows to
collect the metal bits, but I don't know if such gadgets were
around in Bill's day.

Bill tried to teach me that farming is a business, that
animals die, that sometimes veterinary care is too expensive,
and that on a farm, every penny counts. But that didn't stop
me from playing nursemaid. Every few hours I slipped into
the field to check on Bossie's condition, sponging the flies
from her eyes with a wet cloth. Her breathing was heavy,
her eyelids barely flickering when I stroked her chocolate

brown muzzle. After dark, I returned with a flashlight. She was down. Her sides were still, her eyes glazed and staring. Bossie was dead. I removed the leather collar from around her neck and tucked it into my back pocket, a memento I would keep for many years.

The next day, the truck came to haul Bossie away. I didn't go out to watch, and I turned the other way when it passed by the house, heading down the lane to the highway. Now behind in his chores, Bill hailed me to the barn. "If you're still thinking about that cow, it's time you stopped," he said. "This is just the way it is." I picked up the hay fork. I was still miserable, but I knew he was right.

If I had tender emotions towards animals, that's where the softness ended. By summer's end, my body was hard muscle, my shirt sleeves straining around my firm biceps. And I had a voice that could holler home the furthest field of cows.

"Good lord," my mom said, when, back in the city, I answered the phone with the bellow of a bull. "Do you have to talk so loud? You're not calling someone in from the barn, you know."

The following summer, I was invited back to my field of Jerseys. But I turned the job down when I heard there was another baby. Not a calf, a puppy, a colt, or a kitten, but a human baby.

"You may not want to come back since your duties will involve more babysitting than farm chores," Bill's note read. I guess he noticed my preference for mucking out stalls to cleaning up the kitchen.

Months later, I heard that Bill signed on for another agriculture student, and this time he got his young man. I also heard this boy wasn't nearly as good as "that girl" he had the summer before.

Chapter Four

A home is
like a soft
blanket—
warm, cozy,
and secure.
After years
of roaming,
I was eager
to turn our
house into
a home.

A New Home

Mom and I spent three days driving the winding back roads west of Calgary, searching for a home where we could launch a new adventure. Earlier that year my dad had died of cancer, prompting my mother to pack up, move west, and join me in laying a claim to rural life. Agitated by a city's nervous energy, we combed the countryside for our own piece of land where neighbours would be more than five steps away, where cattle drives would have the right-of-way, and where an open window would greet a chorus of night creepers.

We ruled out dense bush—too depressing and not enough light. We also crossed off pancake prairie—too much wind and too few trees. And forget those tidy four-acre plots—even a pair of chickens couldn't survive on something that small.

"And don't show me anything that's called Estates," Mom said. "I don't want to be part of some cul-de-sac development. I want to be off on my own." To say my mother is something of a lone wolf would be stating the obvious. She has never run with a pack, preferring instead the solitude of home territory.

We had taken a pass on just about every real estate listing within commuting distance of Calgary, but we kept looking, enjoying the exploration and the anticipation. Late one Sunday, turning east off a paved secondary highway, we fell silent as the car banged and rattled along a gravel road pitted with potholes. Around each turn we were greeted with a vista of valleys prickly with spruce trees, soft with grazing meadows, and wild with deadfalls and swamp. Then, out of nowhere, a red-tailed hawk swooped over the hood of the car, its wings within inches of feathering the windshield. Like a mirage, it vanished, swallowed by the orange afternoon light. Raptors are powerful omens, and I took this as a sign of good things to come.

We were now sidewinding through a narrow valley, where aspen thickets ambled down gentle slopes and willows dipped their toes in a slender creek. The close hills were a weave of dark towering spruce and open fields thick with belly-deep grass. What a beautiful little valley, I thought. Not a building in sight, just hillsides speckled with cattle, their white faces shining in the afternoon light and their bristly tails twitching at bothersome flies. This was the high country, and I felt the wilderness tapping my shoulder.

Rounding a sharp bend, we spotted a For Sale sign at a gateway leading to a home burrowed in the bush. A small red barn crouched in an overgrown pasture, next to a neglected paddock circled by a weathered and peeling, white plank fence. Rising from the long orchard grass and nodding purple-headed thistles was a cattle chute, its floorboards still intact from a time when it shook under the hooves of range cows.

"Oh, my gosh," I whispered. "Quick, back up the car," Mom said. "I think the home is log." Straining to see through the tangled jungle of matted aspen leaves, we could see filtered light bouncing off honey-coloured timbers. The house grew out of the landscape, its square corners rounded by spruce boughs, ferns, and baneberry. Finally, here was a home that suited its surroundings and did not scream self-importance. Its warmth enveloped us like a cozy feather-lined nest, just as our northern Ontario cabin had done before.

After scribbling down the realtor's phone number on a scrap piece of paper, we inched along in silence, looking back down the valley, where the creek wandered like sinew through sedges and willow. Here was the privacy we were looking for.

By the time I called the realtor, I had convinced myself that such a picturesque place was probably beyond our budget.

"How many acres?" I asked.

"About forty-five."

"Forty-five acres?" I gasped. "Gee, I don't know whether I should bother asking the price, but go ahead. Tell me."

Mom watched as my face went blank. The asking price was lower than any other home we had viewed! At that time, no one was interested in a large chunk of marginal land, much of it best suited for ducks, beavers, mosquitoes, muskrats, and other bog-loving creatures.

Over the next two days, we visited the property three times. We walked trails flecked with the mottled light of aspens, their leaves showing the first hints of autumn yellow. We explored the creek and its many springs, delighting in the discovery of ancient wooden cattle troughs. Their decaying sides were speckled with orange and green mosses, and small trees sprouted from soil that had settled in the rotting bottoms. The fields were dappled with blue asters, silver-green sage, brown-eyed Susans and pink wild roses. A pair of mallard ducks paddled on a beaver pond, its sizable dam indicating the work of several beaver generations.

Kneeling on the hillside was the log home, its beams as straight and strong as coastal totem poles. Large windows overlooked the marshy meadow where does, their fawns hidden in the tall ungrazed grass, gathered in the early evening to nibble on tender willow buds. This was a place where herons came to fish, and where cool rains gave rise to mists curling like smoky swirls in an Emily Carr painting.

Uphill from the house, the simple red barn housed two dirt-floor box stalls, a bevy of mouse nests, a wooden saddle rack, and a tack room where insulation hung in ragged tufts from the ceiling. Several wasp nests dangled from the rafters. Inside, the air was heavy with dust and neglect. The barn was lonely, its stalls longing for a friendly nicker and the sweet perfume of fresh hay and used saddle leather.

We made our final visit in early evening, when daylight and dusk join hands and everything is bathed in mauve.

"What's that across the field?" I asked Mom, having spotted a flash of dark movement.

"Looks like a horse and colt," she answered. "Are you

sure?" I asked. Its size suggested something larger. "Look how it moves. Look at that gangly gait," I added. "That's a moose. A moose and its baby."

Mom and I smiled. At that moment, we knew we had found our new home. We had come home to the land, a place that echoed our past. Here we would relive old memories and make new ones.

Chapter Five

Sweet Surrender

I could live with a wood stove and oil lamps but, like most women, I would not fancy returning to the days of outhouses.

The first year on our patch of paradise I spent alone. I assured Mom I could handle the homestead while she returned to Ontario to tidy up personal matters. I was a kid of the bush, so adapting to country living should be as easy as changing from hiking shoes to rubber boots. After all, we weren't exactly roughing it; we had electricity, heat, and running water.

The cats, all four of them, and I spent a glorious first week in our new abode. What joy to open my window at night and hear the great grey owl hooting down the valley, to rise in the morning to a coyote choral concert, and to watch the boreal and mountain chickadees line dance across our deck. What a privilege to feel cool night air after a day of scorching heat, and to lie in bed and watch the moon slide across the sky, its silver light silhouetting the pointed firs. I had found heaven down here on earth.

And then one morning disaster struck. Turning on the kitchen tap, I received not a drop of water. There was much spewing and spitting, but it was a dry cough. I turned the tap off, and then back on again. Nothing. With the record-breaking temperatures that sweltering summer, I thought the worst.

"Oh no, the well's gone dry," I muttered. "I knew we should have had it tested before moving in."

Counting in my mind how many jugs of bottled water it would take to fill the bathtub and toilets, I began to panic.

My first country mishap, and I was falling to pieces! Darn it, if only I could be sure the creek water was safe, but with beaver ponds, grazing animals, and who knows what dead beasts floating in log-jam debris, it would be foolish to use the brackish water.

Again, I tried every tap in the house. Not a drop. I wonder what it costs to drill a new well? And what will I do if they can't find water? Maybe there's a local water-witcher. My mind was racing with various scenarios, most of them disastrous. The foothills are notorious for erratic layers of subterranean rock. Drill a well in one spot and water gushes like Old Faithful. Move thirty feet over and the hole is bone dry.

Opening the kitchen drawer, I thumbed through the jumbled lists left behind by the previous owner. Furnace repair. Legal land description. Emergency numbers. Septic cleaners. A livestock waterer manual. Ah, here it was, the phone number for a water well company.

"So, does the pump still have pressure?" asked Sam, the young man on the other end of the line.

"How can I tell?" I asked.

"Well, what does the meter say?"

"The meter? Where's that?" Sam replied with a thud of silence.

Our waterworks were in a tiny room in the basement, a maze of pipes running every which way and connected to such gadgets as iron and sediment filters. There were red knobs, blue buttons, and black dials—all Greek to me. I steered clear of this room, avoiding it like I would an ornery bull cornered in a pen.

"Look, Sam, would you mind dropping by? I just moved here, and I really need a lesson in how all this stuff works." Hearing a sigh, I began to beg like a spoiled pup.

"Sam, I know this is a pain, but I'll take notes, and that way I won't need to bother you again." I knew my career as a journalist would come in handy—if you don't know something, just ask a zillion questions and write everything down, even if it's in shorthand chicken-scratch.

"All right," Sam said. "I'll be out some time this afternoon."

It took Sam five minutes to size up the situation; it took him less than a minute to size up me. He was dealing with someone who didn't know a well pump from a septic tank.

"Well, there's your meter, and it's showing pressure, so you know it's not your pump," he said. I studied the small clocklike fitting. It looked innocent enough.

Unscrewing the casing for the sediment filter, Sam scrunched up his face, his hands now covered in grit and sludge. My water was dammed because the filter installed by the previous owners was too small; it could not have strained a drop of rain, never mind gobs of mucky goop.

Wiping his hands clean on umpteen sheets of paper towel, Sam suggested I pick up a bigger filter, available in most hardware stores, he said. I started to fidget.

"Don't you have any with you?" I asked.

"No, they're back at the shop."

"Well, I'll pay you to go get them, then drive back to put one in for me." Sam stared at me in disbelief. What strange breed of city slicker was invading his country?

"Look, I know this is crazy. But really, I just need you to do it this once. Then I can do it myself. I promise." I could see Sam starting to calculate his overtime, recognizing the deal of the century.

My course in Waterkeeping 101 went well. Sam taped shut every valve I was never to touch, and labelled every hose, while I stood by smiling and nodding, and taking copious notes. With the proper filter installed, we turned on the valves. "Counter-clockwise," I scribbled. Water gushed forth, wet and precious. Delicious. Nectar of the gods.

My confidence began to bud. But I still wish I had enrolled in a fix-it program instead of home economics, where I was taught how to boil an egg and sew a shoe bag. Nothing truly useful, like welding, mechanics, or woodworking. One thing about the country—nothing is static. It's either rotting, overgrowing, sick, falling down, dying, leaning over, flooding, or drying up.

And sometimes it's just plain stinky, like the unsavoury odour that had me running around and splashing Javex on everything in sight. I began to suspect our home was a funeral parlour for neighbourhood mice. Within days of moving in, I discovered several of the dead critters squished in traps hidden behind the gas furnace. Why the previous owner had not emptied the traps beats me. Actually, she told me that during their two years in the home, she never saw one mouse. Egads, did that mean these mice had been resting in peace for more than three years?

My dead specimens were deer mice, those sweet white-bellied rodents that the headlines had been warning us about. Beware the carrier of the deadly hantavirus! Touch their droppings, inhale the air, and I could be infected with a disease that would riddle me with muscle aches, a cough, and shortness of breath. Gee, that's how I felt every time I cleaned out the barn!

Doctors were advising anyone handling the mice or their droppings to wear protective clothing so, feeling rather silly, I pulled on a pair of cold, clammy rubber gloves and a nose-and-mouth dust mask. I plucked the shrivelled rodents from the traps, then scrubbed the concrete floor with disinfectant. How come this kind of stuff is never written up in those glossy Martha Stewart magazines? After all, if this isn't country living up-close-and-personal, then what is?

Next, thinking that mice had succumbed in the air ducts, I flooded the heating runways with Javex, but every time the furnace came on, there it was—that putrid smell of something ripe and rotten. I began to ignore it, thinking the dead body would eventually dry out, dry up, and stop reeking.

Then one day, while a neighbour and I were walking around the outside of the house, I was whiplashed by the foul fragrance. I looked at Ralph's face, but he just kept chatting. Surely he must smell it. Maybe he's being polite—but he didn't even wince. Finally, I interrupted. "Ralph, don't you smell something? Something rotten?"

"You mean that smell right here?" he asked, surprised I bothered to mention it at all.

"Yeah, that," I said. "It reeks, like rotten eggs."

"That, my dear, is the smell of a septic system. On warm days like this, you'll sometimes get a whiff, especially if the wind isn't blowing much. It comes out the vent, and sometimes you get a downdraft."

I looked down at the ground, trying to hide my blushing face. I decided not to share my tales about tracking down mystery mice with a jug of Javex. Since then, I've been told to drop a dead gopher into the septic tank, just to keep the good bacteria active: a sort of super supplement to boost its health. I have to admit I haven't followed up on that one, but I do occasionally douse the furnace room drain with a pot of water to keep the backdrafts at bay.

Having survived my initiation into country living, I no longer find it necessary to talk about septic smells. I accept the quirks of the water well system and the trespassing of an occasional mouse. Call it a sweet surrender.

Chapter Six

I have always thought coyotes were better suited to their Aztec name, coyotl, which carries an echo of their musical yodels.

She Who Runs with Coyotes

Having read late into the night, I was looking forward to a slow-footed morning; just one more hour in bed, napping and snuggling with the cats while the thinning darkness of pre-dawn drifted by my window. But there it was again, that lone coyote barking up a storm. I love a symphony of howling coyotes, but this stray was cheeky. There was nothing musical about his song, just a staccato of yips and yaps. It sounded like he was standing outside my window, beckoning me to come hither. Before long, he had every dog in the valley barking the same annoying chorus. Reluctantly, I crawled out of bed, mumbling to the cats to keep my spot warm. "And stay off the pillow, you guys, because I'm not going to be gone that long."

I opened the screen door and squinted into the grey light. There was the occasional star and a phantom moon, but no coyote. I picked up the walking stick leaning against the logs just outside the door, a straight and sturdy pole with a metal tip, a crude spear for driving off cougars and bears. Well, not actually. Anything larger than a porcupine could snap it in half with one playful swat. Maybe I could just try to scare this critter off by calling myself Woman Walking With Big Stick!

28

As I headed to the barn, where I thought I heard the coyote still teasing me with his love call, I called out, "You can't hide from me forever, you know. So come on, get out here where I can see you."

Rounding the corner, I caught a glimpse of his grey-brown coat. I expected him to run off, but instead he held his ground, barking sharp yips and scratching the dirt with his front feet, all the time staring right at me with piercing amber eyes. I struck the ground hard with my stick and then waved my arms over my head, trying to look like a threatening predator. But he stared back, as if amused by my antics. Or was it my get-up? In my hurry to pursue *Canis latrans*, I hadn't bothered to pull on any pants. So here I stood, brandishing my big spear in a nifty pair of powder-blue longjohns tucked inside knee-high black rubber boots. Overtop the matching blue undershirt I wore a tattered green military jacket. Lord knows what I must have looked like to any beast or human passing by.

I thought of my neighbour who drives the schoolbus, hoping he wouldn't be making an early run, his cargo of young faces peering from the windows while pointing their fingers and laughing at the crazy woman. Make that Crazy Woman With Big Stick. Rural communities thrive on gossip, and I didn't need to further fuel the burning phone lines.

I could already hear the niggling voices: "Not even been here a year and she's already going crazy. That's what comes of keeping to herself. I told you she should get more involved. Imagine, a woman living there on her own. It's no good."

I wouldn't normally fuss this way over a coyote. After all, this was his turf too. But he seemed rather aggressive for an animal that usually slips into a dip behind a hill whenever it sees people. Seeing him so close to the barn, I also worried about Mamma Cat, a feral calico that used the shed as her personal bed and breakfast. She was a masterful mouser, and I wanted to keep her around.

After tossing a few small stones towards his pointed muzzle, I watched the coyote scamper off, but then he stopped, looked back, and barked. He began to dig again. And then he squatted, leaving a puddle of urine to trickle in the loose dirt down the hill.

Was this some declaration of war? Was he expecting me to fight for this hill? I thought of Farley Mowat and his book *Never Cry Wolf*, in which he describes how he marked his campsite by urinating on nearby bushes. No way I'm doing that. My barn's on this hill; I've staked it as mine. This was one dominant coyote, but I wasn't about to submit. I was not going to cower or roll over on my back.

The coyote continued to stare, waiting for me to make my next move. Aboriginal stories speak of the coyote as a trickster, a mischief-maker who can change shapes. He can either help or deceive humans. Maybe this wasn't really a coyote. Maybe I was disturbing something sacred. Was I standing on Native hunting grounds? I thought about these hills and valleys inhabited long before the ranchers arrived with their cattle, horses, and barbed wire. Or maybe this little brother was fighting for the spirits of all wild animals lamenting the loss of territory, crowded out by homes, roads, and oil companies that consider no piece of land sacred.

I stared back at the coyote, my green eyes looking into his yellow ones. I'm sorry, brother. I don't know who or what you are, and I wish you no harm, but you must keep your distance, from me and from others like me.

A chilly mist hugged the valley and tugged at my flesh. I was growing cold. Then I sneezed. A big one, a mighty blast that shook the valley like gunfire. As I looked up, the coyote's rump disappeared into the bush. I sneezed again, and he retreated deeper into the shadows. Little brother heard my message.

As I made my way back to the house, hoping to find my bed still warm, I crowned myself queen of the hill. But I also detoured into a grove of saplings, where no one could see me from the road, not even a schoolbus full of kids. And there I pulled down my blue longjohns and squatted. "Just in case," I said. "Just in case the trickster comes back."

Chapter Seven

Like most donkeys, mine love to back into you. They're not getting ready to kick—they want you to rub their rumps. A good tail massage settles the most nervous of donkeys.

Donkey Love

I had yet to meet a donkey, but I knew I wanted one after reading Marguerite Henry's delightful *Brighty*, the tale of a scruffy burro wandering the cliffs of the Grand Canyon. As a toddler, I even had a donkey pajama bag. It was scarlet red with the biggest blue ears any donkey has ever seen. They were held up with stiff wire, but I bent one into a drooping flag just to make him look different. Ever see a donkey in torrential rain? Believe me, their ears droop!

As an adult, I cherished Derek Tangye's books about Minack, the flower farm on the rugged coast of England's Cornwall, where he lived with his wife, Jeannie, a score of cats, and their donkeys, Penny, Fred, Merlin, and Susie. Derek died in 1996, but he left instructions for Merlin and Susie to be sent to England's Donkey Sanctuary, where they are being cared for until their death. The Minack chronicles honour nature, solitude, and animal companionship—the very things I hold dear.

And of course there was Eeyore of A. A. Milne's Winnie-the-Pooh books, though I've often felt Eeyore was too gloomy to be a real donkey. The ones I've rubbed ears with are anything but downcast. They're comics, full of mischief, spirit, and merriment.

About a month after I moved to the country, my neighbour Lyle dropped by to see how I was doing. Studying the place with a friendly but critical eye, especially the paddock where the thick grasses were creeping halfway up the barn door, he made a suggestion that would forever alter my days here.

"You know, you really should get that pasture down. It's a bit of a fire hazard."

I stood in silence, surveying fields that had not been grazed in two years. Besides being dry tinder for a grassfire, it also gave the place an unkempt look, as if no one lived here. Only the small barn was visible from the road, and it stood empty and lonesome.

"I think I can help you," Lyle said. "I've got two donkeys that I'll loan you." Donkeys? Real donkeys? I was thrilled, yet hesitant. Here was another dream coming true, but the reality of having living, breathing livestock on the place also scared me. What special care do donkeys need? How will I know if they are sick? What if they get out? The what-ifs tumbled in my mind, leaving me blithering an excuse about why I couldn't accept Lyle's donkeys.

"That's so nice of you," I said. "But I was thinking of just taking a scythe to the grass. I'm not really set up for animals yet."

Lyle shrugged his shoulders and smiled, too polite to ask what else I needed to house donkeys. I had a barn, fences, a paddock, a livestock waterer, and fields of grass, rosebushes, and thistles. Everything a donkey dreams of.

Lyle looked down, scuffing the ground with the toe of his boot.

"Sure, scythes are good," he said. "They'll do the job."

That night, I phoned my friend Mary. She lives in the city, but grew up on a farm in central Alberta.

"I was offered donkeys today, but I turned them down. I think it's too soon for that responsibility. What do you think?"

There was silence at the end of the phone, followed by a giggle or two. Mary thought I was nuts. She also thought Lyle must think I was nuts. "Why sweat it out with a scythe when you can have animals do the work?" she asked.

"I don't think it would be that hard to take care of a couple of donkeys. You've got water, you've got lots of grass. I'm sure they'd be OK."

I got off the phone and went downstairs, where my books were still stacked on the floor. I found *Brighty of the Grand Canyon* and Derek Tangye's *Donkey in the Meadow*. I flipped through the pages, smiling at the drawings, as I had done so many years ago. A real donkey—I could have a real donkey.

I phoned Lyle and apologized for my irrational behaviour.

"Bring the donkeys," I said. "It'll be fun."

"No problem. Just give me a few days to catch them and then I'll bring them over."

Like an expectant parent, I rushed about, preparing

to receive my two charges. I swung open the barn doors and cleaned out the mouse nests. I filled a stall knee-deep with sweet-smelling shavings. I scrubbed the livestock waterer. I checked the fencelines, removing fallen trees and tightening sagging strands. I bought curry combs, brushes, mane and tail combs, insect repellent, a hoof pick, and a bag of carrots. If they had sold donkey receiving blankets, I would have tossed one in.

And then the big day arrived. It was 28 August, my birthday. My friend Barb was over, and I was just about to serve my homemade chicken stew when the doorbell rang.

"You expecting anyone?" Barb asked.

"Not that I know of."

I wiped my hands on the dishrag and went to the front door. Seeing Lyle's face through the small window, I thought it strange that I hadn't heard him drive down the lane. When I opened the door, I was greeted by a beautiful black donkey. Lyle had parked his truck up by the barn, walking the jenny down to the house as a surprise.

"Oh, she's gorgeous," I cried. "And she's so big."

This was no miniature donkey. What stood before me was a reincarnation of Brighty, a large donkey with a white muzzle, raccoon eye rings, and a silver belly.

"And what is your name?" I asked, my fingers tickling her chin.

"Her name is Sally," Lyle said. "The other one is Cisco, and I'll bring him over tomorrow."

"And what does Sally like best?"

"Hugs," said Lyle. "She likes lots of hugs."

It was a birthday I will never forget. I kept going

to the barn to see if it was true, that a donkey was now living in my meadow. And of course Sally was still there, cropping the shoulder-high grass, her big ears flicking at the flies. Even the barn was smiling. Perhaps for the first time, I really felt like I was living in the country.

Chapter Eight

Longview, Way Out West

Having been raised on cowboy music—I can still hear my dad yodeling "My Swiss Moonlight Lullaby"—I take great delight in living in the geography that shaped such classics as Ian Tyson's "Four Strong Winds." Every year, when autumn begins to turn the field grasses red and the aspen leaves yellow, Mom and I head south to Longview, where Ian packs them in at the local community hall, just a crow's call away from his ranch.

The East Longview Hall sits in a field on a tight curve of highway in the middle of nowhere. Established in 1927, it's a simple structure but a grand one compared to the original Pig Pen Hall, so nicknamed because it was built using the stalls from a hog barn. On this given night, the field outside the hall is a parking lot of pickups, the trucks lined in a row as if they were tethered to a picket line. There are out-of-province licence plates from British Columbia, Saskatchewan, and Montana, and even a few from Ontario. There's something about hearing a Tyson concert in the midst of cowboy country; it's as if his ballads are playing to the ghost riders and cattle phantoms still roaming the

A friend flies in from Ontario twice a year to take in the Longview Hall concerts with Tom Russell and Ian Tyson. We stand outside for an hour to be among the first inside for front-row seats.

37

coulees, as if their spirits are gathered on the porch, catching the musical tributes drifting through the crack beneath the door.

Outside the hall, the sky is a riot of colour: a rainbow of mauves, limes, oranges, reds, and yellows smeared across a heavenly canvas. It's what Ian would call a Charlie Russell sunset, in honour of the western artist who roamed the foothills' valleys, painting scenes of longhorn cattle, dew-soaked cow camps, shaggy buffalo, and lean cowhands. The hills twinkle with amber lights from farmhouses and barns, and a strong breeze sweeps down from the mountains and across the cottonwood flats. This country, with its yellow plains, accordion-folded hills, fescue grasses, and blustery, snow-eating chinooks, is home to the working cowboy. Ranchers have settled here since the turn of the last century and their families still live here, riding the same trails over summer ranges dotted with elk and deer. History echoes up the valleys, where robbers hid out, where whisky runners stashed their goods in hidden shacks, and where Harry Longabaugh, alias the Sundance Kid, worked as a cowhand. This is fertile fodder for many of Ian's songs, and it is the backdrop for Longview, one of my favourite places.

About a half-hour's drive south from our place—double that if the snow is blowing sideways—Longview is a humble village, kneeling at the toe of a steep hill with an eagle's view of sawtooth mountains that stretch south to Mexico. To be here is to be Way Out West. When visitors arrive and want a glimpse of real cowboys, this is where I bring them, promising a snorty remuda of pickup trucks with scruffy stock dogs hanging their heads over the tailgate. The ranches sprawl beyond the cliffs above the Highwood River, and golden eagles spiral and tumble on the winds that whip the rocky outcrops.

The Longview area has starred in such blockbusters as *Legends of the Fall* and the Oscar-winning *Unforgiven*, but it remains a shy celebrity, proud of its smallness. One day I walked into the village post office and asked how many people call Longview home. "About 310," the woman said. "Somebody thought it was 306, but I don't think so." I waited for her to laugh. Surely she wasn't serious about haggling over four people, but her mouth remained as straight as the town's main street.

Folks in Longview take their home to heart, and so they should. After all, this is the apple of Alberta, its collection of frame buildings called Little New York during the 1930s oil boom. A few fields over were Little Chicago and Little Philadelphia, oilfield communities built around tarpaper shacks. During those heady days of gushers and dance halls, Little New York flourished, with butcher shops and barbershops, a dry cleaner's and a theatre, confectioneries, machine shops, and an ice-cream parlour all lining its rutted dirt roads. Today, the Twin Cities Hotel, open for business since 1938 and still honouring the names of Little Chicago and Little New York, stands as a landmark of the town's past.

After the boom, most of the oil-related businesses shut down or moved on, but the ranching families stayed, their names as western as Owen Wister's *The Virginian*, the classic novel about a cowboy who worked at the Bar U Ranch, just a few hills south of Longview. There are the Cartwrights down along Pekisko Creek, the Bews on the banks of the Highwood River and Sullivan Creek, and the late Guy Weadick's Stampede Ranch on the sunlit flats west of Longview. In 1912, Weadick founded the world-famous Calgary Stampede rodeo. Boasting one of the largest remaining tracts of native grasslands in North America, this is ranching country at its best.

As for the village of Longview, it's a town that's on the way to somewhere else. The people who work here don't say much unless asked. But miss the stop and you miss a cast of characters. One warm fall afternoon, I stepped inside the town's tack shop and began chatting with its owner, Wyatt Barett, who whispered that he was making a saddle for actor and polo enthusiast William Devane. Across the street, Wayne Grouett builds stagecoaches and bronze-artist Janet Blackmore, a woman who's as comfortable wearing cowboy boots as she is touring New York's finest art galleries, runs the rustic One Horse Gallery. Up the road is Memories Inn, where a red vinyl chair used by Clint Eastwood hangs from the ceiling and where the walls are a photo gallery of other famous faces who have dined here—Paul Newman, Sam Elliott, Jon Voight, Meredith Baxter, Morgan Freeman, Richard Harris, and Gene Hackman. Just east of town lives Scott Hardy, one of North America's finest silversmiths, whose belt-buckle customers include Garth Brooks, Dwight Yoakam, Alan Jackson, and Andre Agassi. Down the road is rancher John Scott, a professional wrangler who promotes Alberta's scenery as one huge Western movie lot. He's mustered livestock for *Unforgiven, Little Big Man, Shanghai Noon, One More Mountain, Buffalo Bill and the Indians,* and *Lord of the Rings,* and in his early days, he doubled as a stuntman for Roy Rogers and Patrick Wayne, son of the swaggering Duke.

One of the town's most recent additions is Ian Tyson's Navajo Mug, with its diamond willow railings and adobe-coloured exterior, where you can buy a cup of Gunsmoke or

Outlaw coffee, view prints of Charlie Russell's paintings, and pick up Ian's music tapes. The Navajo Mug is itself a fragment of history. The 1909 steep-roofed café was once a one-room schoolhouse as well as a stopover shelter for cowboys driving cattle north from Montana. Its wooden floorboards have also felt the stomping feet of a church congregation and the heeled boots of a saddlemaker. Ian now owns the building, naming it the Navajo Mug after his popular song "Navajo Rug." Longview, which he fondly calls "a dinky little town," has been his home for the past twenty-five years or so. His ranching neighbours faithfully fill the Longview hall to hear him sing songs about their way of life—stories about Spanish mustangs, wet saddle blankets, rodeo riders, and sagebrush-scented winds. The concerts are organized by T & D Productions, the dynamic duo of Twylla, Ian's wife, and Delilah Miller, who owns a bridal shop in nearby High River. It's a hoot to buy your concert tickets there, politely leaving your shoes at the door and tippy-toeing among satin gowns and crisp, black tuxedos.

Back at the hall, the evening is old, the concert almost over. Ian is singing "The Gift," his tribute to Charlie Russell and the land he painted. Outside on the porch, an old border collie waits patiently for someone inside. The stars have punched holes in the coal sky, and a moon hangs high on the horizon, pouring its light on the willows in the sleeping coulees. Ian worries about losing these rangelands to development, but at the same time he's optimistic that the western way of life will always be here, as long as there are cattle to cowboy and horses to ride. I hope he's right, because I always want to think of Longview as being Way Out West.

Chapter Nine

I love to sketch horses in a storm. They stand with their tails tucked between their legs and their heads lowered, the fury sifting around them.

A Horse and a Half

Sally and Cisco were enchanting, living up to their reputations as delightful donkeys and cunning guard animals. As soon as the sun peeked over the neighbour's barn, Cisco greeted the day with his baritone bray. It came from deep in his belly, his diaphragm heaving as his nostrils flared. Opening his canyon of a mouth, he would grumble a few grunts and then inhale, all the time building pressure. Then he'd let go, bellowing like a bull in a field of cows. You could hear that bray more than a mile away.

I soon pitied the dog or coyote that ventured too close. A horse may flee from a dog nipping at its hocks, but a donkey is fearless, chasing its quarry beyond the fence or rearing up to strike it dead with a blow from its front hoofs. Believe me, size matters little. Many times I rescued month-old kittens that strayed from the barn into the donkeys' paddock, and one day I watched in absolute horror as Hud, my blind cat, innocently wandered into longears' territory. Sally and Cisco pretended to graze, but their eyes were fixed on this intruding feline. As I scrambled under the fence, Sally broke into a trot, her mammoth head only inches from the ground as she approached her whiskered prey. I screamed at Hud to run, but to where? He was blind. He couldn't see. Poor Hud, he zigzagged across the paddock, bumping into trees and fence rails while trying to find a way out. Now both donkeys were in pursuit. Hud kept darting from left to right, as if he were dodging a bullet, but the donkeys cornered him, pinning him against a fence plank. As Cisco reared, poised to strike like a deadly snake, I shouted a blood-curdling "Noooo!"

I don't know how Hud found those precious spare inches, but he did, mashing himself between two fence boards beneath the cattle chute. It was like watching a mouse flatten its body to squeeze through a dime-sized hole. Scaling the fence, I ran to his side, lifting him into my arms. His aged body was shaking and his heart was pounding, but his limbs were intact.

It is said a donkey won't kick unless it knows it can make contact with its target. If that is so, then Sally and Cisco were only out to give Hud a scare. They gave me one, too!

With these two warlocks, it wasn't long before I noticed our fields empty of coyotes. It's not that they moved out, they just learned to walk on the other side of the fence, beyond the donkeys' reach. Finally, the days of dropping my pants to mark my turf were over.

Sally and Cisco were easy keepers, their bellies growing round and their coats turning black and glossy with the summer grass. I brushed them daily, grooming deep into their ears where nasty bugs liked to bite. Surrendering to the massage, their lower lips would droop like a bloodhound's ears, and their eyes would soften with the gentleness of a morning mist. There's nothing like having a few donkeys to soothe frazzled nerves, their mañana philosophy rubbing off on the owner.

I offered to buy Cisco and Sally, but Lyle needed the extra money they brought in. Cisco was well known in these parts, passing on to future generations his charm and magnificent bray, and Sally had many years ahead as a breeding jenny.

"Do you have anything else for sale down there?" I asked, having yet to visit Lyle's Old-MacDonald-style farm, where he kept horses, pigs, ducks, goats, sheep, and an assortment of cattle.

"Well," he said. "I've got a couple of mules."

"Mules?" I asked. "How old are they?"

"One's over a month. The other was born about three weeks ago."

I didn't know a darn thing about mules, other than that they were half-horse and half-donkey, but I was tickled by the thought of owning one. These were the marvellous animals I had watched haul wagons of borax on *Death Valley Days*, a popular program in our home in the days of gathering around the black-and-white television with our Saturday night plate of pork and beans. Somewhere, tucked away in a cardboard box, I have a model of that famous mule train, and on my laundry room walls are two tin signs advertising 20 Mule Team Borax. I even have vintage videos of Francis, the Talking Mule.

They were amusing animals, all right, and I loved their Roman noses and cornstalk ears, and when they yawned they looked silly, like moose, but what I knew about them could fit in my back pocket. Ignorance isn't a good thing to pack along when thinking about buying a mule. If I had known then what I know now, I would probably never live with one, but then my life would be so dull.

The day I dropped by to check out Lyle's mules, I found a pretty little red baby peeking at me from behind the rump of her horse mother. Coy but curious, she was absolutely gorgeous, a genuine heart-stopper.

"Her mother's for sale too," Lyle said. "If you're interested, that is."

The mule's mother was a ten-year-old liver-chestnut Morgan mare. She had small, perky ears, a white blaze running down her nose, and a sweeping mane and tail. Under the sun, her dark coat shone like polished jet. Her name was Crocus, as she was born in early spring, when fields are dotted with those wonderful harbingers of warm days to come.

The other mule was small and wispy, the offspring of Ebony, Crocus's mother. Both mule foals were sired by Cisco, the donkey jack now living in my fields—I nicknamed them the Cisco Kids.

With a sea of equine faces studying me, I stared back, wondering whom to choose. Should I take home one mule, two mules, or a mare and her baby mule? If I lived in Kentucky or Tennessee, mule advice would be as close as my next-door neighbour. Down there, longears outnumber horses. Their hardiness first attracted the attention of American President George Washington, who requested that donkeys be brought over from Spain so that mules could be bred to haul goods and work the land. To this day, the southern states are flush with mules, but up here, too many people view them as mongrel jokes: clowns, troublemakers, a stubborn beast that would sooner kill you than look you in the eye.

Ignoring the guffaws, I resorted to books and magazines, reading numerous articles about who should and shouldn't buy a mule. Never owned a horse before? Then a mule is not for you! Short on patience? Then walk away fast! Everything I read advised an inexperienced rider to stick with a bomb-proof horse that's been around the corral several times, a horse that has seen it all and done it all, and thus won't bat an eyelash at a hulking grizzly bear, a dropped rein, noisy trucks, flying plastic bags, or flapping raincoats.

Mules, the articles said, are blessed with more brainpower than they deserve. They love mental games, deciding on their own what to do and when to do it. If you ever punish a mule, it will harbour ill feelings until the day it kicks back. Determined to do things their way, mules even live to the ripe old age of forty, just to saddle you with years of grief. Yes, indeed, a calculating and conniving animal!

Hogwash, I thought. I'm sticking to my guns. Deep down inside I believe few animals are born bad. If handled confidently and with respect, and if not forced into uncomfortable situations, most are willing to please. Somewhere along the way you strike a deal; you become part animal, and they become part human. You start speaking each other's language and you learn to respect each other's space.

If I brought home a young mule, why would it grow up wanting to kick me between the eyes? If I treated it right, why would it carry a grudge and strike me dead years later? It just didn't make sense, so I forged ahead, my will as granite-hard as that of the animals I was about to welcome into my barn.

In the end, I went for the package deal, choosing Crocus and her red-headed mule foal. I figured I could ride the mare while training her baby. I was bringing home a horse and half-a-horse, or as I began to say, "a horse and a half." It wasn't quite a mule train, but it was a good beginning.

Chapter Ten

Roping Lucy

My decision to buy Crocus and her mule colt was the easy part. Now came the hard work. The mare had had some professional training, but the mule had yet to feel the touch of a human hand. Born beneath a star-speckled sky and on a bed of cool grass, she was a wild thing. During the day, she raced with the herd, a small string of four dark horses moving like a train across the vast meadowland.

One moment the horses would be grazing like contented cows, only to freeze a second later when the leader, a coal-black gelding, tossed his head, his ears perked forward and his nostrils open to the wind. He would spin, breaking into a choppy gallop, then extend his legs to swallow more ground. The rest of the horses followed, racing across the flats, up into the bush and circling back through the scrub willow. Who knows what set them off—maybe a scent in the air, a snapping branch in the bush, or just an ancient desire to race the wind.

Shadowing her mother, my molly mule ran on spindly but strong legs, her four hooves a blur in the long grass. The horses whinnied and snorted, speaking to one another while throwing their heads and wind-braided manes. Such freedom: no bridles, saddles, or riders, just horses moving together like a finely tuned orchestra. Their

Lucy and the donkeys have a special greeting for new visitors. They tug their clothing, demanding a scratch between the ears. Brats!

47

gaits were rhythmic, in two-beat trots, three-beat canters, and four-beat gallops. No wonder the horse has such a history with military bands. If I closed my eyes, I could hear the music written to match the different strides, the tempo intended to quicken or slow the band's march.

The gelding led his herd in one more circle, then eased into a trot. Breathing hard, the horses returned to eating, a chorus line of lowered heads. The mule never strayed far from the mare, still playing hide-and-seek behind her mother's rump if she thought I was watching too closely. If we were to become friends, our work had to begin soon.

Having read about imprint training, where owners handle newborn foals within hours of birth, I knew I was three weeks too late, but it was still worth a try. If I could rub and stroke the foal, just like Crocus did, she would learn that fingers poking in her mouth, tickling her nose, or running down her legs were not a thing to fear.

So over the next few days, my little molly mule—named Lucy after that special northern Ontario lake where I bonded with so many wild and wonderful creatures—trembled her way into the world of humans.

Ideally, she would have been penned with Crocus, so I could earn her trust without forcing her to come to me. Like most young animals, she would have been curious: tentative, yet eager to investigate my baggy shirt sleeves, my shoelaces, and my loose hair. It would be a poke-and-prod game.

Unfortunately, that isn't how things happened. Lucy was roped, learning a harsh lesson in forced constraint. While Lyle let her race around the rail corral, I stood and watched, my anxiety shared by a worried Crocus, who eyed the action from outside the pen.

I was amazed at the strength and determination in one so young. Panicked, Lucy circled the pen faster and faster and then scrambled up the rail sides, her tiny hoofs digging in like a veteran rock climber. Before Lyle had time to gather the slack on his rope, she crested the top, her belly now teetering on the creaking rail. In one mighty leap, she tumbled to the ground. I held my breath, fearing one of her slender legs was broken, but in seconds she was on her feet, her eyes wide with terror. Her world was crashing, changing into a world where humans did bad things.

Back in the pen, Lucy began to sweat heavily, her fuzzy coat wet with nerves. The horses were now standing next to the corral, sniffing the air and smelling her fear, their nostrils flared like an open flower. I called time out and put Lucy back with her mother for a well-deserved suckle and tender nuzzle. I wanted to call it a day, but I knew if this session did not end on a positive note, Lucy would become impossible to catch.

While Lyle left to do chores, I returned to the corral, where Lucy now stood dry and relaxed. When I kneeled down low, Crocus wandered over for a good sniff. We chatted quietly, and I purposely ignored Lucy, rubbing the mare's neck and scratching those itchy spots under the jaw. Out of the corner of my eye, I saw the mule stretch her neck towards me. Again, I ignored her, giving all the attention to the mare. Lucy's ears tilted forward, her nostrils twitching. She was now stretched like a giraffe, her neck straining forward with her front legs not budging an inch. I wanted to reach out to her, but I knew better. This had to be on her terms, and I was delighted to see she was trying to trust after such a terrifying start. On this high note, I called it quits.

The following day, I repeated my slow approach. Again, the mule sniffed, her nose only inches from my body. She then stood sideways, so I brushed my arm against her shoulder, like the mare would to reassure her. She tensed, then relaxed. I repeated this several times until she accepted my physical contact without a twinge. Within an hour, I was wrapping my arms around her, massaging every part of her body, except for her ears and legs. I didn't want to rush into handling those long ears until I had her full trust. Handle the head wrong and you risk an ear-shy mule jerking its head high at the sight of a bridle. Those sapling legs also require special care. Like horses, mules bolt from danger, so they don't take kindly to someone grasping their leg.

I ended the day with Lucy's head cradled against my stomach. The sun dipped below the spruce; the day's heat turned quickly to an evening chill. I began to hum a Stan Rogers sea shanty, rocking back and forth from one foot to the other to keep my toes warm. The mare's head dropped, her eyes half shut. The mule, her red head still buried in my sweater, breathed deeply. She was sleeping. This is exactly how I wanted her. Trusting, relaxed, her breathing slow. Her body swayed with mine, back and forth, back and forth, like a tiny boat bobbing on water.

The following weekend, Lyle moved the mare and mule to my place, their new home. They travelled in the back of his pickup truck, the mare's ears almost touching the top of the stock racks, with Lucy leaning against her mother's shoulder.

"Are you ready for this?" Lyle asked, smiling, as we unloaded the two down the cattle chute.

"Guess I better be. There's no turning back now."

I began to whistle another Stan Rogers ballad, only this time it was to calm my nerves. Lucy and I were about to begin our dance, our waltz on water.

Chapter Eleven

Country Fairs

Fair day is full of excitement, like a swarm of honey bees hovering over a clump of fragrant clover. Animals are meticulously groomed, their coats silky sleek and their hooves glossy black. Young riders, some of them so small they could walk under their horse's belly, are braiding manes and tails with red ribbons, and polishing silver bridles until they shine like moonlight on water. Inside the barn, there's a cacophony of crowing roosters and bleating sheep, and rows of lop-eared rabbits and spotted guinea pigs huddled in their cages.

There's a spicy sweetness to the air, a blend of frying bacon, fat sausages cooking on a grill, fresh bread, and robust coffee. Weaving through the crowds are bright-faced children, screaming that they just won a ribbon in the drawing competition, and that their mom's chutney was named the best. And did you know that Jim's photo of his Red Angus bull just took first prize? And poor Jenny, her pickles didn't win again this year. Oh well, there's always next year and the year after that.

I love a good country fair; they are as much a part of the landscape as a good hip-roofed barn. Everyone—young, middle-aged, and old—comes out to celebrate their neighbours' accomplishments and to cheer on the friendly competition. City folk in search of simple

The one bad thing about country fairs is that none of the home baking is for sale. All those prize-winning goodies, and not a free sample to be had.

pleasures also flock to the fair, perhaps remembering their trips to Grandma's farm for Sunday supper.

I may no longer be able to buy unpasteurized cream in a glass bottle, but a fair still paints numerous scenes from the rural handmade life: hardworking farm wives selling fresh eggs, jars of saskatoon-berry jam, stacks of blueberry pies, bags of potatoes, bundles of onions and carrots, knitted woollen socks, gay quilts and floral arrangements, and pastoral paintings of life outside the farm kitchen window. Husbands parade cattle in front of scrutinizing black-jacketed judges, who size up bovine udders, testicles, hooves, and backbones. In the next field, sons and daughters prod and poke their calves, tugging on the leads as their animals shuffle around the 4-H ring. There are always a few tears shed when a champion steer or lamb is sold for slaughter—in some cases, a soft-hearted neighbour buys the animal so the youngster knows it will continue life in the pasture down the road.

Around the cattle pens, the men jaw away the day, talking about their latest calamities, the weather that is always too dry or too wet or too cold, and cattle prices that are never high enough. One old-timer, his hands thick as bear paws and his legs as lean as matchsticks, is bemoaning the cost of pickup trucks. "Was a time when you could buy a nice new one for two bulls," he muses. "Now, you'd have to sell ten of your best." His gripe is met by a chorus of nodding heads, as boot toes scuff the ground, sending puffs of dust over the worn leather.

Fancy machinery may have replaced horse-drawn ploughs, but at our local Millarville fair, which has logged almost one hundred years, the horse pull remains king. A salute to a time when horses tirelessly worked the fields, the competition packs the bleachers with fans waiting to cheer on their favourite gentle giants. The teamsters, holding smooth leather lines, cluck to their horses, setting in motion a mass of muscle. Leaning into their harnesses, the animals drop their heads and drive forward, their back haunches rock-hard as their hooves dig into the ground. Onlookers shout and hoot, as the driver cracks the air with a "Git up there, Jim and Bob." Just as the teams are matched in size, so are their names, with pairs like Belle and Bess, Mitch and Mike, and Hank and Henry. Old farmers leaning on canes, their shoulders slightly rounded, begin to hear voices from their past, the grunts from the horses and the sighs from children who used to walk behind the teams, heaving rocks and boulders onto the stone boat. They love to tell their stories, and I am always eager to hear them.

Throughout the summer, I attend different country markets, selling my art and photography. Men with russet faces, their brows shadowed by farm caps, wander over and study the mule pictures, smiling at the ones where the manes consist of real strands of hair that I have pulled from Lucy's tail. Their lined faces grow soft as they tell their tales of harness heroics: horses that worked faithfully from dawn until dusk; teams that braved blizzards to find their way home; mules that stopped pulling on the dot of noon because they knew it was quitting time; a team that went out of its way to sidestep around a fallen child; and a pair of Roman-nosed molly mules that craved watermelon.

If Grant McEwan were still with us, he would be cheering the loudest and telling some of the best stories. A huge fan of the horse pulls, he grew up when horsepower came in a harness, not in a motor. Born on a Manitoba farm, he went on to become dean of agriculture at the

University of Manitoba. He was also a politician, serving as Calgary's mayor and Alberta's lieutenant-governor, but his passion was the western farming heritage, honoured in the numerous books he wrote.

I recall an interview I did with Grant after the publication of his book *Heavy Horses*. He spoke of the horses like a father would of his son—with deep respect, admiration, and love.

Grant cherished the bustle of the Millarville fair, and I can still see him standing there, his smile stretching as wide as the sky when he visited the heavy-horse judging ring or took in the "Sheep to Shawl" contest, an event that evoked memories of a bygone age. After the sheep were shorn on the back of a wagon, teams of weavers competed to see who was the best at carding, spinning, and weaving the wool into a shawl, with points awarded for speed and workmanship.

Much as country fairs conjure up yesterdays, they also open a window on tomorrow, with young farmers taking the reins from their parents. Let us hope that the family farm survives so that we may all share in the excitement of fair day, watching another generation of 4-H'ers primp and preen their charges, their fingers crossed for a blue ribbon. They deserve our applause, since they are the ones who will be growing the food that our grandchildren put on our great-grandchildren's table.

Chapter Twelve

Flies in the Soup

I have yet to read a book about rural living that does not mention a war with flies. I have yet to read one in which the flies surrender.

Living in the country means living with flies here, there, and everywhere. In the house, in the barn, in your eyes, up your nose, in your mouth, in your butter, and in your tea.

Our windows are often a maze of bumbling flies, butting their tiny heads against the panes, trying to escape into the outside world where they belong. Some years are worse than others, the black mass on the window so thick it threatens to block out the sun like a midday dust storm. Turn on a bedside lamp and they knock around inside the shade, ricocheting off the sides like a crashing race car careening off concrete guardrails.

After several buggy summers, we no longer pay much attention to the pests, waving them aside without missing a word of conversation. But it wasn't always that way. At first, we blamed the bloated fly population on our log home, a natural haven for spiders, wasps, moths, and various winged and crawling insects, but then we visited the neighbours' homes, where half-dead flies were casually brushed from the table moments before dinner was served. Satisfied our own invasion was not personal, I began doing housework while casually humming that old traditional folk tune, "The Blue Tail Fly."

It's not that we didn't try to terminate the bugs, but after a while we too felt like bottled flies, butting our

55

heads against the impossible. We hung yellow sticky strips, but what's a few dozen stuck flies when you're battling hundreds? Anyway, the buzz of them fighting to unglue their legs is unnerving. Same thing for the electric zappers: there's no such thing as a peaceful evening if you're sitting ringside at a fly electrocution. Next came the hanging bag of liquid fly bait, a fatal attraction that smells of rotting fish. After a month, when we counted only two drowned flies, we disposed of the floating nooses. We could have used infrared cameras to detect gaps and cracks used by the flies, then held an open-house caulking party, or hosed the place down with an insecticide, fumigating ourselves in the process. But why bother? It's much easier to accept the wee beasts.

Besides, if you have livestock and manure, you have flies, a licorice all-sorts bag of horn flies, deer flies, stable flies, horseflies, cluster flies, and face flies. When the swarms turn into dense clouds, I buy mesh fly bonnets, snipping the tops off the ear pockets so they will fit over the mule's and donkeys' antennalike appendages. It's rather odd to watch them prance about with their faces covered like partying masqueraders, but it keeps the bugs out of their eyes and prevents them from rubbing their jaws raw on fence posts.

Some guests, however, aren't as cavalier about such buzzing mayhem. Nancy was one such guest. She arrived for dinner after enjoying a drive in the foothills on a beautiful day in the fall, a time when the trees are trimmed in gold and the cooling air is bronzed with autumn light. It's also that time, just before winter lands, when the flies go dopey, bumping into things, flipping onto their backs while their feet pedal the air, and dropping dead for no apparent reason. I usually diagnose a bad case of concussion and dehydration.

Toiling in the kitchen, Mom and I ignored the overhead buzzing and graveyard of dead flies lining the window ledges. But not Nancy.

"What's with all these flies?" she asked. "I don't remember them being like this before."

"Yeah, it's been a bad year," I said. "But it's no big deal. They'll disappear in a few weeks."

It was obvious my insouciance did not rub off on Nancy. Chatting away, she kept waving and grabbing the air in front of her, whether there was a fly there or not. Her jerky movements were more distracting than the circling flies, but I said nothing, figuring things would improve once we sat down to eat. Wishful thinking on my part, because the opposite happened.

Just as I slipped a spoon into my bowl of thick soup, a fly dove from the overhead light, plunging headfirst into the steaming broth. After a few short backstrokes, he died, his black body draped in creamed turkey. I looked over at Mom and began to laugh. I didn't dare look at Nancy. Picking the fly up by its wet wings, I stuck it on my side plate.

"Oh well," I said. "That's one less to deal with."

After that, Nancy continued to drop by for short visits, though not too many, and never at dinnertime.

Our insect collection, however, amazed children. My nephew in particular entertained himself for hours, standing at a window with the fly swatter in his hand, poised to strike. This wasn't virtual warfare. It was the real thing, and much more practical than a zap-boom-bang computer game. Mind you, once he left, our windows needed a good scrubbing to erase the battlefield of smeared guts and tacky yellow goo.

The best weapon is truly a vacuum cleaner. In the fall, we don't bother putting it away, parking it instead next to the large sunlit windows where the flies play tic-tac-toe. Turn it on and within seconds the buzzing is muffled, as zillions of flies disappear down the tunnel into a dark cave cluttered with paper clips, dog and cat hair, caps off ballpoint pens, and stray twist-ties. Mom usually stuffs a wad of newspaper into the nozzle, so that the flies don't play survivor games, wending their way back from the cave and up the tunnel to daylight.

Most country people don't talk about the flies, unless it's to predict incoming rain. When thunderheads start stacking up like massive buffalo humps, the flies start sticking to everything—crawling along our arms, drinking from the corner of our eyes, and clinging to the mule's face. For some people, however, the pests are one more reason to pound in the For Sale sign. One couple, who were moving for a multitude of reasons, from the lack of services to the harrowing winter commute into the city, panicked every time potential buyers arrived on their front stoop. All they could do was hope and pray that the flies kept quiet during the walk-through. What the visitors didn't know is that moments before their arrival, the owners had fired up the vacuum cleaner, sucking the flies off an upstairs window that was impossible to see through because of the buzzing black cloud. Maybe flies should be included under the rules of real estate disclosure, or perhaps rural municipalities should stamp on land titles that all residences are under an existing flight path, because there's no such thing in the country as a No Fly Zone.

Chapter Thirteen

Curse of the Open Gate

Leave a field gate open and you've got trouble on the run, merry hooves taking flight, exploring roadways, backyard gardens, and anything else off-limits.

I could see the yawning gap between the fence post and the gate as I drove down the lane; the chain was unhooked, its links dangling loose. My stomach churned. The animals, usually loafing around their water tank and salt block, were nowhere in sight. I slammed my foot on the brake, the sudden stop spitting gravel across the grass. Throwing open the door, I launched myself into a quick jog, thinking—hoping—that they were grazing in the coolness of the valley. But who was I kidding? Stick around when there were nasturtiums to stomp and striped sunflower seeds to steal? Jumping back into the truck, I sped to the house, looking between the tree trunks for any sign of Crocus, Lucy, or the donkey. If my stomach twisted at seeing the open gate, it sank when I spotted a gaping hole in the back deck. Lucy must have clip-clopped her away across the rotting and sagging platform, then plunged through, leaving tufts of red hair snared in the sharp and jagged splinters.

I hadn't run a sprint since high school, but I'm

While driving down our road, I have been met by escaped bulls, cows, donkeys, and horses. Never far away is a frantic owner, trying to catch the animal before a disastrous collision.

59

sure I broke a personal best as I raced through the fields, terrified I'd find her crippled with a broken leg. Scrambling up the woodland trail, I cursed the roots I stumbled over and the trees that blocked my view. If I was in Saskatchewan, they could run for three days and I'd still see them, but not here, where folded hills close like a curtain. Down the hill and through the heavy bog I went, stopping to catch my breath and to look for hoofprints or fresh manure, or anything to indicate I was on their trail. My mind took me places I didn't want to go. There was no fence on the other side of the creek, just miles of dense bush so thick I would never find them. If only I had tied a bell in Crocus's tail! I pushed on, traversing the hillside and then huffing up the last steep slope before our western boundary.

There, trotting back and forth along the fenceline, was Crocus, her head bobbing over the strands as she chatted with the neighbour's gelding. Trailing behind, on four strong legs, was Lucy—thank goodness! Sally the donkey, who knows no word for harried, was up to her nostrils in ripe grass. Now all I had to do was halter the mule and donkey and let Crocus follow. Halter? What halter? I couldn't believe it. In my hurry to find the animals, I had left the halters hanging in the barn. I trotted the half-mile back, then returned at a lazy jog.

I don't know why I didn't halter only the donkey, knowing the other two would tag along. I guess it would have been too easy. Instead, I stumbled downhill, dragging along a pokey donkey on one side while trying to hold back a frisky mule on the other. Meanwhile, Crocus stayed behind, hiding in the overgrown bush. If my charges weren't playing tug-of-war with my arms, they were forging ahead like two plough horses, forcing me to lean back, my heeled boots scraping two furrows in the ground. If I lurched forward, my shins smashed into the pencil-sharp beaver stumps that littered the hillside.

By the time we reached the last meadow, I was bruised and exhausted. Lucy and Sally, however, had settled, and I could see Crocus following the ridge like some war-party scout. I took a deep breath and began to think about a long, hot soak in a lavender bubble bath. I was half-submerged in the sweet-smelling water when my bubble burst. The mule crow-hopped, almost jerking my left shoulder out of its socket. Sally surged forward like an attacking battleship. High on the hill behind us was a herd of elk, at least a dozen of them headed our way, and fast. Exploding from the bush, Crocus, who hates elk, was charging towards us at a full gallop. Lucy, sensing danger and wanting to join her mother, reared and then jumped ahead, burning the rope across my palm. I let her go and watched her vanish across the field, her back leg kicking at the rope dragging behind her. I held onto the donkey as if she were a raft in a storm. When Sally and I arrived back at the barn, there was no sign of Lucy and Crocus. I retraced my steps, but I couldn't find them.

In less than a hour it would be dark, and Lucy was loose with a dragging lead. If her halter caught on a sharp branch, she could break her jaw. Her rope could snag a windfall. I looked for hoofprints in the mud, but only the elk had left tracks. I shook a bucket of oats, hoping they could hear the sound that usually brought them running from the field. No such luck. One more look, I thought. I'll just check the barn once more before I phone the neighbours to let them know I had two runaways.

I peeked through the open barn door, expecting to see empty stalls, but just to prove me wrong there was Crocus, picking at some loose stalks of hay, with Lucy at her side. Other than the splashes of mud stuck to their legs, they looked as if they'd been back for hours. I removed Lucy's lead and halter. Stroking her ears and face, I checked for any swelling between her knees and fetlocks. She had a small gash from where she'd gone through the deck, but otherwise she was fine.

I shuffled back to the house, but not before checking all the gates. I still couldn't remember leaving that gate open. I looked back at Crocus, suspecting she was my Houdini. Lyle had warned me she had a way with latches and hooks, toying with them until they opened. If only she could talk! Knowing Crocus, she'd deny everything, blaming the entire fiasco on the donkey.

Exhausted, I skipped dinner and went to bed, preferring my pillow to a warm soak. Lying there flipping through a magazine, I began to giggle at the evening's misadventures. Talk about the Keystone Cops! Then, outside my window, I heard a long nicker. It was Crocus. I laughed, and she nickered again. My little lock-picker, determined as always to have the last laugh!

Chapter Fourteen

Celebrity Fence Posts

Before I moved to the country, Emmet sent me a book about a bull moose that courted a Hereford cow. I have since seen many moose grazing from cattle feeders, the tame and the wild living in harmony.

"Well, Martha, what do you want for your birthday? You're turning forty, so I've got to get you something."

"No you don't, Emmet," I said, hooking the phone under my ear and laughing at his calling me Martha, a nickname he'd plucked from Hollywood's dusty Westerns. I'd met Emmet Walsh, an actor, several years before on the set of *Killer Image*, a movie being shot in the Calgary area. We hit it off and have been friends ever since.

Back in town for another film, Emmet was being his usual generous self, offering to buy me all sorts of goodies. But I couldn't think of a thing I wanted. I didn't need jewellery—earrings can be ripped from your lobes if they catch on sharp twigs or brush—and our window ledges were already crammed with coloured bottles, sun-catchers, and china animals. I didn't have space for one more book, I didn't own a CD player, and I sure as heck wasn't going to let him buy me clothes.

"Look, Emmet, seeing you again is good enough. You don't have to get me anything," I said.

"Aw, come on now, there must be something you need."

I thought for a long moment, the phone awkwardly

cradled between my neck and shoulder as I doodled a donkey face on a message pad.

"How about something for the ranch? You must need lots of stuff out there," he said.

Emmet was onto something. Since my move to the country several months before, I had spent more money at the hardware store than I had at the grocery checkout. I'd love to meet the person who said country living was simple and cheap: the lucky sod obviously inherited everything, including the kitchen sink. Whatever savings I had for the little extras were disappearing faster than a gopher with a coyote on its heels.

Every week my list grew longer: salt blocks and salt block holders; mineral blocks; feeding pails; hooks for the barn; rings to tie the donkeys to; wire-cutters; barbed wire staples; nails, in every size they make; fly stickers; insect spray for the mule and donkeys; a hoof pick; curry combs; soft and hard brushes; hoof glue; more fly stickers; halters, in different sizes; more nails; rope; bits and bridles, in different sizes; a saddle; a saddle pad and blanket; wasp spray; ant dust; tick and warble powder; and a trunk to put it all in. And that was just for starters.

Yes, there was something Emmet could get me, it being my fortieth and all.

"Come to think of it, Emmet, I could do with some fence-building tools. I want to put in a new stretch of fence, but I haven't got what I need to do it."

"Well, OK. So where do we go for something like that?" he asked.

"There's a place in Calgary, not far from where you're staying," I said. "It's called the UFA."

"The U-F-A?" he drawled, dragging each letter out, as if the high altitude was stealing his breath.

"Yeah. It stands for the United Farmers of Alberta. It's a great place. They've got all sorts of neat stuff."

"Then let's do it," he said.

Going anywhere with M. Emmet Walsh is an adventure, especially in the back forty of Alberta, where people struggle to put a name to his familiar face and voice. I've never seen Emmet asked for a handshake or autograph, yet he's one of Hollywood's top character actors, having appeared in more than two hundred movies and television shows, including *Ed*, *The X-Files*, *NYPD Blue*, *Bonanza*, *A Time To Kill*, *Blade Runner*, *Blood Simple*, *My Best Friend's Wedding*, *Brubaker*, *Slap Shot*, *Raising Arizona*, *Serpico*, *Reds*, *Ordinary People*, and *Midnight Cowboy*. He plays good guys, bad guys, and everyone in between, his rumbling voice as distinct as the eye-patched pilot he played in *Snow Dogs*. He turns heads, but few in small-town Alberta can place him, and even if they could, fewer would plague him. Their cheers are reserved for the volunteer fire crews and local rodeo stars, not for silver screen celebrities.

For several months, there were rumours that Brad Pitt had a retreat down the road, but besides reporters trying to track down the truth, no one seemed to really care. Probing questions were met with a shrug and indifference. A comment would go something like this: "He might have a place around here, I don't really know. But you'll have to excuse me, because I've got a horse in this trailer that needs feeding." Not exactly what you'd call being star-struck.

So walking into the UFA store, where high fashion means a quilted saddle blanket, horse shampoo, and hoof gloss, I could guarantee Emmet there would be no hiding paparazzi. If you want to buy things that will help you get dirty down on the farm, this is the place. Shelves are flush with engine oil, grease, motor batteries, overalls, vaccines, scythes, twine, and barn paint. Out back are stacks of fence posts, planks, rails, railway ties, livestock gates, corral panels, storage tanks, stock tanks, holding chutes, hopper bins, and water troughs.

"Hey, how about this? Got one of those?" asked Emmet, his hearty voice echoing down the aisles as he suggested every item we passed.

"No thanks, Emmet. I've got bedding forks. And I've got pitchforks. And I don't think I need any more rakes."

Instead, I grabbed a shovel with a square-ended blade for slicing through tough and tangled grass, a hand auger for digging postholes, and a heavy mallet for pounding the posts into stubborn clay.

"This should do it," I said, as we made our way to the checkout counter, where again Emmet went unrecognized, even when he signed the credit card receipt.

Since then, I have dug dozens of postholes with those tools, cursing every boulder I hit, every pool of water I strike and every blister I break as the rock-hard clay fights each turn of the auger. But with each bead of sweat, I think of Emmet, quietly thanking him for such practical presents. And when I'm done for the day, I wash the grime off my hands with a bar of French soap from a gift box he gave me several years later, determined, I'm sure, to bring some feminine fragrance to this outfit.

As Emmet likes to say, his foray into the fencing business up here means he owns a piece of Alberta real estate—"Yeah, I own land in Canada," he jokes. "A whole bunch of fence holes."

Don't Name the Ducks

The distant white mound gleamed against a backdrop of frozen brown leaves, the sharp contrast as obvious as the white patch on the rear of an elk. What was it? It didn't move, and it was too bright to be snow. The unusual clump was down by the creek, where spring was beginning to melt muddied snowdrifts

"What happened, ol' girl?" I asked Crocus, my fingers stroking her forelock while my other hand hugged her head close. "What went on here? I bet you know the whole story, don't you, my dark beauty?"

I turned away from the mare's dark eyes, leaving her standing by the barn, its outer walls begging for the promised coat of fresh paint.

"I'm going to check this out," I said to her over my shoulder as I began sliding down the hill, its surface slick with mud and ice. Another day for rubber boots. No wonder they call them farmers' moccasins, I mumbled, looking down at my knee-high green wellies. Purchased years ago in Scotland when I was hiking the rain-soaked moors, they were also handy footwear for the squishy gumbo that greets every farmyard around here come spring thaw.

This was my first spring in the country, and I welcomed

Native to South America, Muscovies are not as tolerant of cold, wet weather as other ducks. But they are a hardy bird, and I imagine that is why they survived a frigid winter in my unheated outdoor pen.

67

the rich aromas of wet earth and new growth. The afternoon sun was delicious, its golden fingers massaging the treetops and melting the last remnants of snow, but as I crossed the creek, the mysterious mound chilled the day's warmth.

"It's her. I just know it's her," I said, feeling a lump in my throat. "After everything I did to get you through the winter, and now you're gone."

At my feet were the remains of Lily, my Muscovy duck. Her quizzical look, her cheeky waddle, her beautiful ivory feathers—all gone. Just her orange bill and clumps of soft down remained, leftovers from a coyote's midday meal. I searched the sky and willows for Martha, my other duck. And then I spotted her feathered tombstone, marking the spot where she gasped her last breath. I looked up at Crocus, who cared less about the crime committed below her hilltop pasture.

"This is what it's all about out here, isn't it, Crocus?" Life and death. Prey and predator. Crocus's natural instincts ran close to the surface, her hooves ready to dig in and her legs poised to take flight at the first whiff of danger. This would eventually become my undoing, but for now, I admired her wildness. After too many years of city living, I was looking forward to my own reconnection with nature.

I know wild animals must eat or be eaten, but that didn't stop me from thinking about the day my ducks arrived, their two heads poking between the slats of their wooden crate. Lyle gave them to me, thinking they were the perfect gift, an easy initiation into farming. I had no experience with poultry of any sort, and figured the powder blue budgie I owned as a child wasn't worth too many beginner's points. I stuttered, warning Lyle I had weasels that would slip through the pen's mesh and murder the ducks. But he was too seasoned for that lame excuse.

"You think you're the only one with weasels?" he asked,

somewhat stupefied by my ignorance. I immediately regretted the comment and decided to listen in silence. We unloaded the ducks and watched them explore their new home, a pen the previous owner had used to rehabilitate injured hawks. I'm sure the ducks would have quacked dead on the spot if they had known the plumage of the former tenants. Satisfied that I now knew the tail-end from the bill-end of my new charges, Lyle climbed into the rusting cab of his truck.

"Just don't go naming them," he said. I forgot his advice as soon as he rounded the first curve in my laneway.

Within a week, my web-footed friends were answering to Martha and Lily. Being a responsible owner, I bought a guide to ducks, but was stopped short when the author suggested Muscovies were the perfect duck for butchering. They were so ugly, he wrote, that killing them was a task without emotion. What nerve, I thought! Lily and Martha aren't destined for a dinner plate. They're pets, following me around like loyal sheepdogs and playing chase with the cats, spreading their wings and hissing at them like gargantuan geese. Like me, Winston Churchill couldn't bear the thought of dining on one of his own birds. Apparently one Christmas he was about to carve the goose when he learned it was one of his own. Refusing to slice the bird, he said, "I could not possibly eat a bird that I have known socially." Well, God bless you, Mr. Churchill!

The tears began to flow as I climbed the muddy hill, leaving behind Lily and Martha's scant remains. In the end, the coyotes did what I could not do. I guess Lyle was right. I should never have named them, but to me there was little difference between Lassie the dog, Flicka the horse, and my pair of tame ducks. No, I was glad Lily and Martha didn't live nameless lives. They had individual personalities and they deserved individual names.

Still justifying my attitude towards creatures meant to be savoured with fancy sauces, I peeked inside their shed, as if they might magically reappear, as if the feathered remains a half-mile away were really those of someone else's ducks. But all I saw was a lonely space where they had once slept, their heads turned and tucked under their back feathers. Their abandoned straw bed sat in the corner, a few strands of down woven into the round nest. Several pieces of lettuce floated in their water dish. I managed a weak smile, thinking about the time Martha took a frigid midnight swim and earned a night's lodging inside my house.

"Look at you, you silly bird. You're frozen. You'll die if you stay out here," I squawked upon seeing her crisp feathers. "You don't go for a bath when it's minus thirty outside!"

Poor Martha! Her greatest pleasure in life was taking a bath. So when the passing of summer took with it the plastic wading pool I had purchased for her daily dunk-and-dive, she began using her water dish. Upon making my final late-night check, I discovered her half-frozen body, her feathers clinking like icicles as she tried to crawl across the wooden floor. Her bill clacked as I bundled her into a blanket. Martha spent the night thawing out in my bathroom, oblivious to the swarm of cats anxiously pacing outside the door. By morning, she was all puffed up and preened, ready to strut her magnificence. I'm sure what saved her was her Rubenesque figure. Back in her shed, she gossiped the day away with Lily, telling tales about nifty indoor bathtubs and flocks of rubber duckies.

This is how I choose to remember Lily and Martha, as two silly ducks who splashed under a big blue sky until their lives ended in the split second of a wingbeat. When the spring storms come, I like to think of them romping in a huge swimming pool in the sky, splashing waves down to earth below.

Chapter Sixteen

When Dreams Turn into Nightmares

The best way to stop a runaway horse is to turn it in a circle, disengaging its hindquarters. Unfortunately, I learned late the importance of training a horse to move its hind end independently of its front end.

My mare Crocus was a wild beauty, her mane a waterfall of waves and her coat as dark as a witch's cape. She had the thick neck and small ears of a Morgan, a breed renowned for its stamina, and her legs were straight and strong. To ride her at a trot was to float. To watch her run was to see freedom.

Freedom—that's what Crocus was all about. Freedom to gallop and graze, freedom to fight, and freedom to turn her back on a human voice. As boss mare, she lived to do as she pleased.

When she came to us, Crocus hadn't carried a rider for five years, not since her thirty days of professional training, just enough schooling for her to learn the basics of stopping and turning on command, and of moving from a trot through a canter. She was what you'd call green-broke, a polite way of saying not a horse for the inexperienced. I know that now. I wish I'd known it then.

I thought my years of riding dude horses would count

for something. After all, there wasn't a vice I hadn't experienced—rearing, bucking, runaways, and barn-sour. But riding other people's horses and owning your own is the difference between walking a plump pony and jockeying a hot thoroughbred. Understanding a horse takes more than stepping into the stirrup of a tacked-up dude horse.

I had good intentions, but they didn't make up for my ignorance. I walked at her side every day, chatting about the clouds above and the earth below, fed her a handful of oats each morning, combed the tangles from her mane and tail, and told her I was her friend. But still, whenever she saw a halter in my hand, she ran like a racehorse leaving the starting gate, playing catch-me-if-you-can. I should have stuck with her, walking her down until she turned and faced me. She needed to learn there was no reward for running away. But foolishly, I grabbed a pail of oats and returned to the field, where she inhaled the grain while tossing her head high above my reach. In less than two minutes, she emptied the pail, trotted down the hill and crossed the creek like a cheeky and rebellious teenager. On many occasions, I stood there dumbfounded, the empty halter hanging in my hand.

I eventually caught Crocus, but only by locking her in the corral when she came in for morning hay. It saved my temper, but taught her nothing. Next came bridling, a war of wits. Up went her head until her ears were poking the clouds, and clamped shut went her mouth until not even a hair could slip between her teeth. So out came the honey, the sweet molasses, carrots, and crunchies, as I bribed her into dropping her head. When she took the treats, I slipped in the honey-coated bit, not realizing she had me right where she wanted me, playing servant.

Maybe if I lunged her, I could reverse our roles. With her circling me on the end of a long line, I could control her gaits and movement, a step towards becoming boss. Lunging looks easy, but I ended up walking backwards with one very confused horse. This time, I was the one who signed up for a lesson.

Steve Turner is a respected horse trainer and had taught Crocus the basics those long five years ago. He didn't remember her, but he knew she'd be rusty from lack of use.

"That animal would have left here barely broke. And she hasn't been ridden since?" He shook his head, staring at me in disbelief. After teaching me the finer points of lunging, he wished me luck, but not before offering some sage advice: "Green horse, green rider. That's a bad combination. You should really have a seasoned horse." I knew he was right, but I tried to shake it off. In the coming days, I would be haunted by his words.

Just give me time, I thought. Crocus and I will work it out. But we never did. I always went to her; she never came to me. Her years of running free as a brood mare left her with little need for people. She spooked if I carried a shovel, if the gate chain rattled, or if my jacket flapped in the wind. I should have read the signs, but love can blind you and, despite our problems, I was in love with her.

Then, one day while I was lunging her, she slowed her pace. The line sagged and brushed her knees. Like a dust devil spinning from the ground, Crocus reared, flashing the whites of her eyes, her body taut. She bolted, charging through the open gate and into the woods. The dragging line fuelled her rage, driving her legs like pounding pistons. I could hear the snapping tree branches and feel the earth shiver as her furious hooves drummed the ground. She raced back up the lane, churning the loose dirt and gravel, and veered when she spotted Lucy, her mule colt, galloping along the fenceline. Blinded by her fury, Crocus never saw the barbed wire, running into it with the force of a tank. The top strand broke, snapped back with a vicious bite, and threw her onto her haunches. Struggling to her feet, she resumed the madness, finally returning to the pasture.

Crocus stood still, her sides heaving and foaming with sweat, her nostrils flared. Approaching her shoulder, I unclipped the line from her halter. She turned to face me, displaying her chest, which was turning red with blood. From her neck to fetlocks, her flesh had been sliced by the wire. I tied her to a post and washed and treated her cuts. The gashes were superficial, but her mental wounds were deep.

Over the next few days, it was obvious Crocus no longer trusted me. With my confidence crushed, she went on the attack, striking me with her front hooves. She trembled when I haltered her and walked away if I approached her. My dream had turned into a nightmare. Crocus knew I wasn't the boss; worse yet, she knew I was scared of her.

One spring day, everything came undone. Preparing for a ride, I ignored her swishing tail and resistance to being saddled. I didn't want to spoil her by giving in to her evasive behaviour. What I didn't realize is that I had been spoiling her all along, giving in to her tantrums when I should have worked her through them.

It was the May long weekend of 1995, the same weekend actor Christopher Reeve broke his neck when he fell from his horse during a cross-country jumping event. I was working Crocus in a trot, but she was fidgeting, rounding her back and ignoring my leg cues. Her stops were usually clean and crisp, but not today. Riding the fenceline next to the road, she nervously quickened her pace. I asked her to stop, but there was no response. Seconds later, she broke into a dead gallop, racing towards the gatepost. I had lost control. I was on a runaway, a loose locomotive.

In those numbing seconds between leaving the saddle and hitting the ground, I felt the grip of death. My forehead struck gravel, my knee cracked on the saddle horn, and the palm of my hand ripped open. I sat crumpled in the lane, watching the blood run down my shirt. My face burned, my knee was twice its normal size, and the trees, grass, and clouds shifted into hues of black and yellow. I had lost my colour vision.

A stranger, who was driving by when he witnessed the crash in his rear-view mirror, was now helping me get up. Limping to the house, I stopped to look at Crocus. She stood there like a wild mustang, her head strong and defiant, her eyes hard. I began to cry. Was it the saddle? Was it the bit? Was she in heat? It no longer mattered. I knew we'd never trust one another. I knew Crocus had to go. Steve Turner was right; we were a dangerous couple.

It took me three weeks to find Crocus a new home. Lyle didn't want her back, and potential buyers were either bucked off or kicked. When it became obvious no one wanted a ten-year-old horse with a bad attitude, a neighbour offered to truck her to the slaughter yard.

One more phone call, just one more, I promised myself. Time was running out, but I had one card left to play. I called Del, the owner of Crocus's sire. He listened to my story and agreed to help. He spent an hour trying to catch her, eventually snaring her in the bush. Crocus fought the rope, pulling back on the tightening noose. I'd read that some horses, mares in particular, will commit suicide rather than give in to capture. Crocus appeared to be one of those mares.

"For a moment there, I thought I'd have to cut the rope before she choked," Del said. "This is definitely not a horse for the novice, but she's a good-looking animal. I wouldn't mind getting a colt out of her."

When Del tried to lead Crocus, she balked, pulling back on the shank. Del stepped towards her rear, snapping the end of the rope on her butt. Without hesitating, Crocus moved forward. When she refused to step into the trailer, he again snapped the rope on her rear. She walked in, realizing she had met her match. Her days of explosive tantrums were over.

Del shut the trailer door. "I'll tell you something," he said. "This horse is not an outlaw. She's just spoiled. She's never been made to do anything she didn't want to do."

I have never felt so guilty, despite Del assuring me that her problems began long before I owned her. I said a quiet goodbye to Crocus, and then watched the trailer rattle down the road until it disappeared around a bend. I never saw my beautiful black mare again.

Chapter Seventeen

Don't Fence Me In

In the hit song "Don't Fence Me In," composer Cole Porter heralds the open spaces of yesterday, when a cowboy could ride a cayuse clear to the mountains without opening a gate. Mr. Porter, you can ride double with me any day—I too long for that era when the only barriers were raging rivers, a chain of mountains, and forests so thick no horse could fit its belly between two trunks.

It's not that I don't think fences are necessary. The problem is, I hate putting up fences. I might like it better if I lived on desert flatland, where the tallest plant was a saguaro cactus and machinery could rumble as the crow flies, pounding in a half-mile of posts in less than a day. But my land slants like an overbite, its slopes strewn with clutches of aspens, boggy springs, and a zillion mole and pocket gopher holes. It eats machinery. So most of my fencing is done by hand, a task that chews my gloves, bites my fingers, and swallows my ego.

There is an art to building a fence. A stretch of taut wire and perpendicular posts, the wind singing in the lines, the evenly spaced uprights as straight as guardsmen, is a masterful sculpture. A good fence defies pushy livestock, spring floods, and wind-drifted snow. Sadly, I have yet to build such a fence.

My first line of fencing should have been a cinch.

Mesh fencing is ideal for keeping small livestock such as miniature donkeys inside their pastures. Unfortunately, even without barbs, it has a mind of its own. I have had many a wrestling match with the cumbersome rolls.

I paced the distance at 120 feet. Only twelve posts and no gates—an easy afternoon's work, or so I thought. It took me more than six hours to hand-auger the twelve postholes. I was fooled by the first two, which went smoothly, but the third one kicked back when I hit a rock halfway down. With my belly pressed to the cold earth, I reached into the dark pit, my fingers probing for a lip, but there was none. I then tinkered with a crowbar, chinking and chipping, but it was as if I had snagged a chunk of Canadian Shield. At a dead end with no detour, I abandoned the hole and began to dig another cavity about a foot over.

This time, no rocks, just a knot of twisted aspen roots snaring and stalling the auger. I climbed back up the hill to fetch a pair of clippers and slid back down with shears, an axe, and a bow saw. This was it, I was drawing a new line in the dirt, and I was armed and ready.

Four hours, three boulders, and dozens of plaited roots later, I was finished. Done in. Exhausted. With gouged arms and blistered palms, I stood back, admiring my twelve deep caverns as if at any moment they would begin spewing rich crude. I should have called it a day, but no, I wanted this fence up by dark. I pounded the posts in with a mallet, jarring my teeth and breaking blisters until my hands were raw. But I was on a roll, and with daylight still edging across the sky, why not do the wiring? Surely this would be easier. Roll out the wire, tap in some staples, and presto, I would be the brilliant architect of a fine stretch of barbed wire, or "bob-wahr" as they say down Texas way.

Well, it didn't take long for me to understand why Texans hated the arrival of this armoured fence. Not only did it end the days of the big ranches by shutting off cattle trails to Montana, it snared animals and then ripped them to shreds, the barbs slashing their legs as they struggled to free themselves. Fierce opposition to these barriers sparked fence wars, with cattlemen cutting homesteaders' fences until wire-cutting was declared a felony. Alas, fencing was here to stay, and today there are more than five hundred patented barbed wires barricading the entire western sky.

One zealous group declared barbed wire the Devil's Rope, and, in my opinion, it's an appropriate name. I have survived a capsizal while rafting the whirlpools and howling white water of Hell's Gate on British Columbia's Fraser River, but that was a mere scuffle compared to the bloody combat I endured in wiring my fence. The moment I snipped the wire from its spool, I released a wild animal, one with fangs that grabbed, punctured, and didn't let go.

Like a venomous serpent, it whipped and lashed the air, its razor-sharp teeth cutting my flesh. It gouged my back, slashed my arm, and bit my hand. The wire was alive, pulsing with horror, an evil creature from the pages of a Stephen King novel. I stomped on it, trying to kill the fiend, but it wasn't until I grabbed it several inches from the end, as though I were holding a snake behind its head, that it settled. If I released my grip, it would again whirl and sidewind, trying to return to its circular coil. I heaved a rock on the end of the wire and hiked back up the hill. In a huff, I rang several local hardware stores.

"What is it to this fencing?" I snapped. "How do you get the kinks out of the wire and get it to stop spinning all over the place?"

Trying to stifle a snicker, the clerk explained that I was missing a few gadgets, such as a fence-stretcher to keep the wire taut. I could almost hear him slap his knee when I told him I was rolling the wire spool along the ground, and not from the back of a truck, the civilized way to string a fence.

"You doing this on your own?" he asked.

"Yeah, it's just me out there."

"Tough job."

"No kidding," I replied.

I did finish that fence, but it's a pathetic sculpture, banned to the bush and fortunately out of sight. The wind can't even pucker a whistle on its sagging lines. I have since built several more fences, all of them sad affairs, with Y-shaped tree branches propping up lazy wires and aspen poles woven between strands to temper the slack.

I had the first posts in for a cross-fence when Ralph, my neighbour, pulled over and suggested I wait until the weekend, when he was renting a fence-post pounder. Do the posts in the boggy area by hand and leave the rest, he said. When Ralph dropped by several days later, he couldn't help but notice how my posts zigzagged like a drunken nomad.

"They're not in line," Ralph remarked.

"Yeah, I know. I'm not sure how that happened."

"Oh well," he said. "I guess we'll call it a drifting fence."

"Sounds good to me," I replied. "Sort of poetic, don't you think?"

That fence was supposed to keep the mule and donkeys from wandering onto the power cutline, but if the creek is low, the mule slips around the corner post, barges through the dense willow like a moose in rut, and flicks her tail as she makes the great escape to the forbidden pasture. You can almost hear her bray a tune about murmuring cottonwoods, starry skies, and those fabulous unfenced spaces. Another Cole Porter fan!

Chapter Eighteen

Tale of Two Dogs

It was the night before Georgie and Maggie came to live with us, and I was as giddy as a six-year-old. Actually, we didn't know two dogs would be moving in, but just the thought of one squirming pup had me dancing in my slippers.

The week before, I had picked out a forlorn, freckle-faced pup, the type every dog book warns you not to buy. She was a scrawny runt, hiding from the world like a hedgehog curled up in a tight ball, so shy she refused to leave her cardboard box. I pleaded with her to step outside and join her sister, who was napping in my mother's lap, but she clearly wanted nothing to do with us.

Always a sucker for an underdog, I reached into the scruffy box and gently picked her up. Her tiny body shook with fear, and she dribbled a stream of urine down the front of my sweatshirt. "That's OK," I cooed, looking into her sad brown eyes.

These were the only two pups left in a litter of border collie and Australian shepherd crosses. They were blue merles, their coats flecked with salt and pepper as if someone had splattered them with buckets of white and black paint. In the sun, their wavy coats had a silver sheen, like a blue roan horse. Looking at their pleading faces, I couldn't believe some rancher was ready to shoot them because they were rangy mutts, not of pure blood.

Australian shepherds did not originate Down Under. They arrived in Australia in the 1800s with Basque sheep herders from the western Pyrenees. When American sheepmen began importing Aussie sheep, the Basques came along with their dogs.

81

The piddlin' pup was no longer shaking; in fact, she was now licking my face, melting with each slurp my initial reluctance about housing a dog who was part border collie. They're wonderful dogs, so smart and so loyal, but I've met too many neurotic ones, crazy from confinement and lack of work.

"They're herding dogs. And we don't have anything here for them to herd. They'll go nuts," I said to Mom. Training them to bring home the mule and donkeys was out of the question. We might as well sentence them to a quick death, what with the mule's murderous eye and the donkeys' lethal hooves. But Mom was missing canine company. When I was growing up, we were never without a dog to bring along its laughing face and wagging tail on hikes and car trips. Many times Mom had mentioned she wanted another dog, but until now we had put it off, knowing how a dependent pup changes a household.

Listening to my concerns about how to collar so much energy, the dogs' foster owner explained that this mix of breeds, while still requiring daily workouts, would also settle for a soft couch. As if on cue, the pup, still cradled in my arms, resumed licking my face, until I was slimed from forehead to chin, until I forgot my fears about owning a stir-crazy stock dog.

Mom was still petting the other pup, a truck of a dog, with a handsome face, square shoulders, and a broad rump. Now we had a dilemma. Which one should we pick—the shy runt with the sweet, rascally face, or the bold, confident one with the white blaze? As usual, we were split on the matter.

"The shy, thin one will probably end up being sickly, you know. She'll need a lot of work," Mom said.

"Precisely. That's why we should take her," I said. "No

one else will want her. No one else will understand her or spend the time to understand her."

My mother fell silent, but I knew what she was thinking. Just what we need, another special needs animal on the place. We already had a blind cat, a colicky mule, a scared-of-his-own-shadow ginger feline, a fat donkey, and a geriatric grey tabby. And now we were contemplating a scraggly, fearful pup.

Well, we didn't have to decide today. We told the foster mom we would return in a few days for one of the pups; we just weren't sure which one.

When the big day came, we were still undecided, so we dropped by for one more look before heading to town with our list of doggie items. Both pups recognized us, and, like the twins they are, they waddled in tandem to the gate. They sat down together, their rumps hitting the lawn at the exact same second. They cocked their heads at the same angle and gave us the same longing look out of equally blue eyes. They dared us to pick one over the other. We couldn't do it.

Mom and I climbed into the truck and drove to town, the silence in the cab filled by our common thoughts.

"We haven't got much longer to make up our minds," I said. "Are we getting one pup, or are we getting two?" No answer.

When we parked in front of the pet store, I repeated the question. "Well, are we buying one leash or two leashes?"

"Guess we're buying two," Mom said. And that was that.

While our decision made for the two happiest pups in the world, it was met by a barrage of criticism from dog experts. Taking two pups from the same litter was a sure way to court doom, they said. Our dogs would never bond with us, only with each other. At some point, they would even turn on one another, like sisters from Hell. Because they were herding dogs, they would run away and join a circus of coyotes, chase cars until one day they were squished beneath the tires, harass the neighbour's cattle, nip our heels, destroy our house, freak out during electrical thunderstorms, and run circles around us until we came to our senses and got rid of them. We ignored it all.

Initially we thought of naming them Kanga and Roo, to honour their Down Under roots, but the cute combination would have a tragic ending if, for whatever reason, we lost one of them. We'd be left with only half the word, a constant and sad reminder of the missing companion. So we named the bold one with the white blaze Maggie, short for magpie, those squawky birds that have a knack for knowing at 4 AM which is the bedroom window. Maggie grew into her name, barking at the break of dawn like her rowdy namesake.

The freckle-faced runt we named Georgia, after the artist Georgia O'Keeffe, a solitary and a radical who loved to walk the desert with her dogs, preferring their company to most people's. Georgia was eventually shortened to George, a suitable tomboy nickname for a dog whose cute face belied a keen taste for grouse, mice, and fresh animal droppings.

They were good pups, only once chewing forbidden items—my leather martingale and riding gloves. I would never have known about the latter, except that I found the uneaten snaps on the carpet in the middle of the mud room where they slept at night. They were true twins, doubling our pleasure and our trouble.

Chapter Nineteen

Mouse Tails and Tales

Deer mice have the sweetest faces. Their eyes and ears are larger than those of most mice and voles, and their white chins give them an angelic look. The deer mouse was Walt Disney's model for Mickey Mouse.

I picked up what was left of the mouse, a disgusting pair of mangled hind legs and a hairless tail. "Yuck, why can't you guys eat the whole thing?" My question was directed to the four whiskered faces now sunning themselves on the back deck: Tristan, Fergus, Hud, and Kip, my feline quartet. Stretched out across the warm wood, they blinked and twitched their tails in perfect harmony. No one was about to fess up to the shredded entrails. "Guess it was a team effort," I said, before tossing the mouse guts into the bush.

When I first began discovering half-eaten carcasses, some of them with only the head missing, I was confused. I couldn't imagine a predator being so wasteful. Who was committing such mutilation? These were gruesome sights, conjuring up images of sacrifices and decapitations in the middle of the night. One day, while I was washing the breakfast dishes, the mystery unravelled. Through the kitchen window, I watched the barn cat stroll up the lane, his demeanour as lazy as trees on a hot summer day. Without a flinch, a leap, or a pounce, he bit what seemed like empty air, but he kept on moving, not skipping a step, his back as straight as a carpenter's square. Curious

85

about what he was up to, I went outside and walked over to where I witnessed the mighty gulp. There, lying upside down in the grass, was the corpse of a copper-coloured field mouse. Its flesh hung red and raw, and already a couple of flies were buzzing over its remains. Less than twenty feet further up the lane, there was another murdered mouse. Again, only the head was missing.

It had been a good summer for the local rodent population. When I walked through the fields of long grass, it was as if the ground was fluid, moving with scurrying mice, moles, and voles. The hawks, owls, and coyotes were having a field day, swooping and pouncing, their efforts paying off with mouthfuls of mice. Obviously the barn cats were also savouring the boom, chomping their favourite cuts and leaving the rest behind, the overstocked buffet allowing them to be selective diners.

My neighbour Lyle, however, had a different take on the matter. "You know, there's a reason why the cats leave the tails."

"Why's that?" I asked, thinking I was about to hear a scientific dissertation concerning the bitter taste of certain body parts.

"Because they use the tails later, for toothpicks," he said, his expression flat as a prairie sky, until seconds later it cracked, detouring into a laugh. I groaned at his joke, finding it as disgusting as the sight of stringy innards, but perhaps there was something to his rib-tickler. My cats are now aging seniors and, along with developing stiff hips and inflamed gums, they have lost several of their teeth. They're built more for comfort than for speed, but if they're lucky enough to snare a mouse, they consume the tail. With gaps in their gums, they no longer need toothpicks!

But in those earlier days, my cats were like tigers, their tabby stripes invisible in the grassy shadows, their bright eyes burning in the darkness. I'm sure they invented their own games, pretending they were sleek cheetahs or long-maned lions. Ready to stalk. Ready to kill. Ready to guillotine some poor wee mouse.

"Nature can be so harsh, so raw," I said to Lyle. "It shows no mercy for the small or weak."

Lyle smiled. He didn't have to say a word, because I already knew what he was thinking. After all, he was the one who warned me about not naming my ducks, only to have me whimper when I found their bodies shredded by a coyote. Now he was listening to me whine about the ruthless murders of meadow mice.

I like mice. I even had one as a pet when I was about nine years old. His back and face were the colour of coffee, and his belly was a soft, creamy white. I called him Rawhide, and he'd run up and down the sleeve of my blouse, sometimes piddling while he scampered between my elbow and wrist. When he died, I buried him in our backyard in a small box padded with layers of Kleenex. The entire family attended the simple funeral, held under a shady umbrella of elm trees that cast filigreed light across the lawn. Such a grand farewell for such a little guy.

So, while I wasn't about to turn our house mice into pets, I wasn't the type to jump on a chair and squeak and squawk at the sight of one scurrying along the baseboards. But I have to admit that the pitter-patter of mouse feet in heating ducts drives me to distraction. It's like someone incessantly tapping their fingernails on a countertop, or the drip-drip-drip of a leaky faucet. Before long, it's the only sound I hear. It drowns out the passionate poetry of Vivaldi's "Four Seasons," the precious strings of Pachelbel's

"Canon in D," and even the boldness of Beethoven. So I was not amused one evening when, minutes after settling into a steaming bath, I detected the unmistakable sound of mouse claws scratching their way through the maze of heating ducts. My orange cat Fergus heard it too. Sitting on the edge of the tub, he stopped dabbing his toes in the suds and looked up at the bathroom ceiling. Hark! The tippy-toeing of mice! With gazellelike speed, he leapt from the tub to the floor and in a flurry raced throughout the house, hot on the rodent trail. Darn! I thought I had taken care of all points of entry, from outside vents to squirrel-chewed holes, but every fall at least one mouse finds a sliver of a crack to squeeze through. Mind you, things have improved since my first winter here, when the mice moved in for a winter conference. I found split sunflower seeds under the stove, in the drawers, under the kitchen sink, in the cupboard, and just about anywhere else the mice could stuff the secret cache they had stolen from the outdoor bird feeders. Over several days, I screened the vents, squirted foam into cracks, and packed steel wool into the spaces around the water pipes. Gradually, our uninvited mice guests all but disappeared, and the few that tunnelled in rarely made the great escape. It's hard to trick four sets of cat claws!

But this Duct Mouse—that's as close as I came to giving him a proper name—was persistent. During the day, he was quiet, but come night, he put on his dancing shoes, tapping out his rhythms along the tin runways. And then, just as I was ready to cross over into a sound sleep, he would head to his private kitchen for a buffet of cracked corn and sunflower seeds, or whatever he was finding down there. He would begin to chew. And chew. And chew. It was like having a woodchuck in your ear.

This went on for a week or so, until one night the cats crowded around a heating vent in the corner of the living room. With their whiskers tense and their tails twitching, they sniffed the air around the register. I stopped what I was doing and listened. I was sure I heard a pitter or a patter from the vent.

"What is it, you guys? Has that mouse finally come up for air?"

I pushed aside the feline audience and lifted the register. Peering down the dark tunnel, I couldn't see anything, so I turned on the light, catching a glimpse of something small. An eye—looking right at me!"

I slammed down the register and jumped back. "There really is a mouse sitting there, and it stared right back. It didn't even move," I said to the cats who were mewing with anticipation, each one bunting the other out of the way. Hold it a minute. It didn't move? Unless it was dead, a mouse wouldn't just sit there. It would at least blink, wouldn't it? With a beaming flashlight clutched in one hand, I delicately removed the register. The mouse was still there and, yes, its red eyes were staring at me, but I laughed as I reached in and held it up by its tail. Dangling from my fingers was a scruffy toy mouse, its eyes scarlet red and plastic. Who knows how long it was sitting there, or how it even got there, since it would be impossible for the cats to bat it through the register's narrow slats. And why did my cats all of a sudden take an interest in that vent, when the only creature on the other side was a lifeless, dust-covered toy?

I don't have the answers to these questions, but I never heard from the Duct Mouse again. Perhaps the mouse was a shape-shifter, turning into a toy to save its own life.

Chapter Twenty

Down by the creek, there is a huge spruce swirling above a bench of duff and needles. It is a lovely place to sit and watch the winter wrens.

Wise Old Trees

My friend Steve eyed the skeletal remains of the ancient spruce, its knuckled backbone still standing years after its limbs had shed their last fingers of needles. Its trunk was lean and tall, reaching towards the sun that gave it life for so many years. Its wood was dry and grey, bleached by years of heat and high winds. Searching for seasoned firewood, Steve asked if he could cut it down. Studying its gnarled skin with reverence, I shook my head.

"No, not that one. It's one of my favourites."

During summer storms at night, I watch that old tree from my bedroom window, its stark branches flashing silver-white as lightning floods the valley, gusts of wind tearing at its trunk. It stands naked and soaked, its boughs no longer there to shed the pelting rain. The following morning, against a glorious sunrise, its arthritic fingers turn pink, orange, and mauve as the new day's warmth stretches along the creek. I think of the life this tree has lived and the wondrous things it has seen. No, this tree is not for the taking.

Steve smiled and moved on; he had long ago recognized my sentimental bonds to the natural world, whether found in heartbeat or heartwood. As a child, I skipped through knee-high snow in search of the perfect Christmas tree, dragging it home through the bush to decorate that special spot in our cabin. But as an adult,

I stopped cutting the Yuletide tree, no longer able to justify ending its life for a few days of celebration. For decades that tree fought for sunlight and water, each year of success marked by a growth ring. To chop it down in mere minutes seemed a callous insult.

Trees are noble creatures, especially in their later years. They're like grandparents, crooked with rheumatoid limbs, perhaps, but with the wisdom that comes from a long life. Dying timber is much needed in our forest society for woodpecker nests, owl perches, and yes, even for its silver beauty. Every summer old trees house families of woodpeckers—hairies, downies, and the enormous pileated woodpecker with its scarlet crest. For weeks, we watch the parent birds squeeze their way through the perfectly round holes they have drilled with their pointed beaks. And then one day a great cacophony vibrates inside the tree truck, as nestlings hatch and squawk for platters of food. Another generation to flit through our valley, hang upside down from our balls of suet, and dig for insects while bracing their tails for balance against the rough-barked trunks.

Long after the woodpeckers move out, the trees' grey limbs provide roosts for great horned and great grey owls, as well as the red-tailed hawks that ride the valley's summer thermals. Standing guard over the marshy valley, the trees offer a crow's-nest view of mice and voles tunnelling through the thick meadow grass

Burro Alley has no shortage of trees, and I do my best to thin the scrawny young aspens that succumb to disease or sneak into my pastures during a drought, but the older ones I leave as forest sentinels. They are seasonal clocks, ticking off changes in temperature and daylight. In spring, their tiny lime leaves are flush with new life, as thin and transparent as the flesh of a baby robin. Gradually, they turn a deeper shade and don wide-brimmed summer hats. Then autumn sweeps in like a magician, turning the leaves into warbling yellow canaries with wings fluttering like a candle before an open window. With the coming of the arctic winds, the canaries take flight, migrating in ochre and russet flocks before dropping to the ground, where they will be painted white with winter's first snowfall.

Trees are timekeepers, not only of the seasons, but of lives. They are memory journals, sometimes seeded when we are born, sometimes planted upon our death. And oh, so many events along the way! Think of the farm children who screamed with glee as they sailed back and forth on a creaking wooden swing, its ropes looped over strong tree limbs. Years later, the same tree is an umbrella over a picnic table where the family gathers for birthday parties, afternoon teas, and harvest dinners. Dozens of farm cats have clawed its branches, and scores of cows have slumbered in its shade. If it's my tree, the donkeys have gnawed on its bark and rubbed and scratched their manes along its lowest branches. A rock sits at its feet, marking the final resting place for the farm dog in the very same spot where he used to dig a hole to escape the summer's scorching heat. The tree becomes a bookmark, a reference point in later years. How many of us, upon returning to our birthplace, observe the trees? We remark, "I don't remember that apple tree being so big, do you?" or "What happened to that old cottonwood down by the river? The one we used to swing from on those hot, muggy days?" We are joyful when we spot our favourite tree still standing mighty, and we are silenced when we discover a special grove bulldozed to make way for another road or home.

With trees housing such a library of change, I never weary of life when wandering along bushland trails. There are orchestras of light and stories of unfolding drama: birth and death unravel on the forest floor.

Tucked in the foothills, where aspen shadows mingle with heavily robed spruce, our home is embraced by trees. Their branches springboard squirrels onto our roof, where I hear them skitter across the cedar shakes. Over the years, we have cleared away those dead trees that threatened to fall against the house, their final purpose in life being to fuel our fireplace. As for the others, we allow muscled chinook winds to play axeman, and when the monsters do topple to the ground, their bellies shelter new homes for burrowing animals. One spring, when the ground was still covered by a crust of ice and snow, I discovered a dead skunk curled up in a hollow sheltered by the roots of a spruce windfall. It looked as if it had died in its sleep, below a roof of snow, in a place where it would become part of the earth.

When the carcass of that silver tree outside my window takes its final bow, it too will return to the soil, and in its place a new tree will take root and begin its quest to touch the sky.

The Raven Lands

It's spring, and the chores are endless. The manure is waiting to be wheelbarrowed to the far field, the livestock waterer needs scrubbing, and the mule and donkeys are due for their annual spring tune-up: vaccinations, worming, and teeth rasping. It's a hectic time for veterinarians. Pens are bursting with sheep ready to lamb, cows about to calve, horses soon to foal—and donkeys, too, that are growing rounder by the day, their babies ending their year-long float inside the womb.

Dr. Wayne, however, squeaks me into his schedule and drops by within the week.

Lucy is always his first patient, though probably not his favourite. Giving her shots is never an easy task: at first, he hides the needle behind his back, using his other hand to pinch her neck skin. This takes her mind off what's coming next, and blocks her view of the approaching needle. With a firm pat, he is done before she can react. Then, wandering over to Sally, Dr. Wayne furrows his brow into a question mark.

"Is there any way that donkey could be pregnant?" he asks, eyeing Sally's ample girth.

"Well, she could be. There was a donkey jack in with her for several months," I said. "But she's pretty young yet. She's just coming up three."

"Oh, that can't be," said Dr. Wayne. "She looks a lot older than that."

"Well, have a look at her teeth. She's just cutting the top ones."

After greeting Sally with a muzzle-rub, he folds back her lips.

"Well, I'll be darned," he says, looking at the two big chompers cutting through her red gums. Donkeys lose their central milk teeth when they are between two and a half and three years old.

I didn't think Sally was pregnant, either. Frankly, I wasn't ready to receive a donkey bundle of joy. When Lyle loaned me Sally and Cisco, I hadn't even thought about the possibility of them having a baby. If she was barely three, she would have conceived as a late yearling—impossible, I thought. That just wouldn't be fair. Lyle hadn't said anything about them breeding, and if they were being intimate, they were doing it out behind the barn, because I hadn't spotted any amorous behaviour. Cisco had since gone home to Lyle's so I couldn't confront him about the matter.

The next time Lyle dropped by, I mentioned Sally's rotund figure. "Just looks like grass belly to me," he said.

"Oh good, because I don't think I'm ready to play midwife to a donkey."

Three weeks later, while brushing Sally's belly, I noticed her udder had doubled in size. Oh my God, what's happened to it? It's big. It's swollen. And the teats are the size of a logger's thumb. Looking blissful, Sally dug into yet another flake of hay. She was eating for two. She was going to have a baby whether I liked it or not.

Over the next few days, I stacked the stall with fresh straw, soft and fluffed, so that when the time came Sally and her baby would have their own private room, away from Lucy. Other than that, I didn't have a clue what to do, so when I arrived home several days later and found Sally hunched up, turning in circles, and mildly kicking at her belly, I was dizzy with both excitement and panic. Either she's got colic or she's going into labour, I thought, as I tried to peek between her back legs. Sure enough, the tips of her teats had spots of milk. I patted her fuzzy forehead and reassured her that all would be well. I told her not to move, to stay put: I'd be right back.

Down at the house, I phoned Lyle for instructions, but his mother answered.

"I don't know where he is, but he won't be home until tomorrow," she said, her bad news sending me into a whirlwind of panic. "Well, what am I supposed to do? This is her first baby, and I don't know how to help her. I've never done this before. Should I call a vet, or just wait, or what?"

"Just leave her alone," said Lyle's mom, in a quiet and collected voice that did little to soothe my jangled nerves. I couldn't just leave Sally and abandon her when she needed me the most, or at least that's how I saw it, so I rang up my neighbour John, who owns miniature donkeys. He sensed the urgency in my voice and was standing in my field ten minutes after I made the call.

"Oh, she's real close. She'll probably have the baby in less than an hour," he said.

Like an anxious father, I paced the fenceline. Sally too was unsettled, moving back and forth between the paddock and the barn, standing up, lying down, turning to look behind her, all the time looking confused, as if she too didn't know what to do.

"You're OK Sal. You'll be just fine. You'll see." I tried to comfort her, but I felt so useless. My instincts told me to boil water and fetch plenty of clean rags, but I just stood there, amazed that our barn was about to be blessed with a newborn.

It was dark now, and I could barely see Sally, except for her white eye rings and muzzle. I was worried. There was no sign that her placenta had ruptured, but if it had, it happened more than an hour ago.

"Maybe I should call a vet. This is taking a real long time," I said to John, who had said little in the last half-hour. His donkey births were usually over in twenty minutes.

"Just give her a few more minutes," he said. "She looks like she's getting ready to lie down again."

Sure enough, Sally flopped on the cool grass. She gave a mighty push, and out popped the tip of a white sac.

"What's that? And why isn't she pushing anymore?" I said loudly, as John rushed forward, grabbed the membrane, and ripped it open. Fluid gushed forth. There was something protruding, but without any light we couldn't make out what it was. It looked grey, as if it could be the rubberlike cap that covers the hooves until after birth. Whatever it was, it didn't move, and Sally just lay there, stretched out, with her sides throbbing. Where was the baby's muzzle?

"Come on, Sal, push. Just one more push," I said, my hand pressed over my own stomach out of sympathy, but the ol' girl didn't budge.

"She's in trouble, isn't she? I mean, she's all done in. She isn't even trying anymore. And the baby hasn't moved at all. I thought that was the nose we saw, but it wasn't, was it? The baby's going to suffocate."

"I'm really not sure," John said.

"I can't stand this," I blurted. "I'm going inside to get a flashlight."

At the same time, John rushed home to call a friend who breeds donkeys. When I returned, Sally was nowhere to be found, but I could hear a high-pitched bleating, like a newborn lamb. Calling Sally, I bounced the flashlight beam across the field. She wasn't there, but from behind me came the same eerie screech. Casting the light in that direction, I made out the shape of Sally, up and wandering around the paddock, a pair of long skinny legs dragging from her rear end. Two little hooves scraped the dirt. Moving the light higher, I could see the half-born donkey, its head now outside mom, its mouth wide open and screaming.

Sally walked over, pushed her damp, sweaty forehead into my stomach, and then looked up, her eyes pleading for help. I began to cry.

"I know, Sally, it's hard. God, I wish I could help you, but I can't." Everything I had read said not to pull a foal unless you know what you're doing. Otherwise, you could risk injuring the baby and the mother. At least the baby's head was out, and it was breathing, bleating, and screaming.

Minutes later, John drove down the lane, just in time to see Sally lie down and give one mighty final heave-ho. Out came the baby, four feet and all, followed by the afterbirth. John stepped forward, felt between the baby's hind legs and then turned to me with a big smile. "It's a jenny," he said. Sally had given birth to a little girl.

Taking a few steady breaths, Sally got to her feet and ambled over to the pasture, where she began to graze as if nothing had happened. Sopping wet, the baby followed. Oh, what a marvellous night! By this time, the traffic was starting to back up along the road, concerned neighbours wondering why we were prowling about with flashlights. Hearing about the newborn, they congratulated me—as if I had something to do with it!

In much need of sleep, John headed home, after I thanked him for possibly saving the little jenny's life. If indeed the baby's muzzle was what we first saw emerging inside the membrane, then John's tearing of the tissue may have unclogged its nostrils and mouth, allowing it to suck in its first breath. Brewing myself a hot cup of tea, I phoned my mom, who had yet to move in with me. It was 3 AM in Ontario, but she still mustered enthusiasm over hearing a baby donkey would be here to greet her when she arrived in three weeks' time. Before going to bed, I returned to the pasture for one last check. A full moon was now overhead, moving across the sky, bathing the field and barn in silver. It was a gentle June night, with bats darting about, a distant dog barking, and the sky a shining lake of constellations. At the centre of this pastoral beauty was the jenny, now nosing her way along Sally's belly, bumping and bunting, searching for her first bit of food. She needed the colostrum, that first thick, yellow milk that flows with protective antibodies. Sally nudged the baby's rear, guiding her to her udder.

While the baby sucked, I buried the afterbirth so it wouldn't attract coyotes. Without a herd to protect her, Sally was on her own. I could have locked her in the stall, but she seemed to be enjoying the cool night air, and the lush grass would help her milk flow.

Rising early the next morning, I phoned my newsroom editor, Ken Hull, to tell him about the midnight miracle. A horse enthusiast himself, he didn't mind that I'd interrupted his breakfast, and indeed encouraged me to take the day off. About a year later, when he retired from the newspaper, I gave him a figure of a donkey as a reminder of a truly important news event.

With daylight creeping around the edge of the fields, I was eager to see the little jenny wake up to her first full day of life. Walking up the lane, I could see Sally in the middle of the field, the baby's legs visible behind her mother. When I spoke, the baby wobbled around her mother's side. One look at her ears and I laughed. They were huge, the size of her mother's, but on such a small head! With a jet-black face and white rings around her eyes, she looked like an alien raccoon, bizarre yet adorable. I expected her to cling to her mother, as most newborns do, but she bounded over to greet me on stiltlike legs that were amazingly sturdy. She sniffed the cuffs of my pants, then wrapped her tongue around a wrinkle, tugging at it like a robin jerking a worm from wet soil. Reaching down, I scratched her forehead, which was a mass of hair, a puffy pompadour with a shaggy fringe. When she didn't mind that, I began rubbing her neck, and before long she was leaning into me, soaking up every kind word and every massaging touch. Something told me this little one was imprinted, a result of my face being the first one she saw while struggling to come into this world. After that, she followed me everywhere, charging around me in circles while throwing out the occasional cow kick. She took to tugging at my clothes, purposely tipping over the wheelbarrow, and braying whenever she heard the bang of the front door that told her I was on my way up the lane.

On the first morning of her life, a row of ravens perched on the crossover beam at the ranch entrance. Swooping down in hopes of finding some birthing tissue, they groaked and clucked, sounding like a scratchy old-time record. I have always had a soft spot for ravens and crows, admiring their intelligence, complex personalities, and glistening plumage. Popular mythology portrays them as prophets, and their presence has always brought me great comfort. They gathered outside my father's hospital bedroom on the morning he died, perched in a single tree that spiralled skyward from the concrete. In the three months he lived there, they appeared only once—at the time of his death. Friends at the other end of the country later told me that ravens had suddenly appeared outside their homes at the same time.

And so, with a bleacher of ravens watching, I blessed this newborn donkey with the name Raven, so that I would always remember the night she landed. It was around then that I christened our land "Burro Alley" as it seemed we were destined to share our lives with longears.

Chapter Twenty-Two

Mule Whispering

Mules are usually sterile, but there have been some cases of mules giving birth. However, I don't think Lucy even comes into heat. Little Peso shows no interest in her, and she doesn't seem to suffer from mood swings, unlike cranky Raven.

Lucy grew into a stocky but good-looking mule. She had a refined face, not too broad between the eyes, with a straight-sloping nose, a sign of a willing animal. Her Mohawk-style mane and small hooves gave away her donkey lineage, but her ears were somewhat cropped compared to those of most mules, and she had the sleek legs of her Morgan mother. As for her temperament— well, time would soon tell. I couldn't control what was hiding in her genes, but I could expose her to all sorts of ghoulish monsters, like dragging ropes slithering through the grass, flapping plastic bags soaring like crested pteranodons, and snapping branches suggesting predators about to pounce. Not wanting her to spook like her mother, who shied at every shadow, I began the education of Miss Lucy.

Always curious, she followed me around as if there was an invisible lead between us. While some days we practised haltering, others were spent lazing together in the pasture: pulling weeds, poking sticks into anthills, or watching the cows across the road. I would rake the manure or stroll along the creek, letting Lucy know we could share time without her having to work. With this soft approach, I was soon able to walk up to her in a twenty-acre field with a halter looped over my arm. Without my having to hide the lead behind my back or inside my jacket, or to offer a bribe of oats, she came to my side for a tickle and rub, then dropped her head so I could slip on the halter. Her reward was freedom, as I would then release her for the day. Equine behaviour towards people is rarely personal, but I have little patience for an animal that flees just because I show up in its field. If I feed, groom, and water Lucy, I expect some gratitude, not a butt swinging into my face and a sprint out of sight.

For the first three years of her life, Lucy and I basically hung out together, with Raven trotting along on our daily explorations. Mom and I would sometimes halter the two of them, then go for a walk into the west fields, weaving through underbrush, stepping over fallen timber, and crossing the creek ditch. They saw deer and moose, smelled bear, and heard thunder—a picnic for the senses.

In a round pen near the barn, Lucy learned to stand tied without pulling back, listen to my voice and verbal commands, walk across a billowing tarp, and accept ropes draped over her body and loosely coiled around her legs. I had her drag a rope in a small pasture, so that if I ever dropped a rein she would not panic. At first, she kicked at it, stepped on it, and backed away, snorting, trotting, and racing around until she realized the winding serpent meant no harm. I did not want Lucy to be like her mother, running into a barbed wire fence because of her rage over a trailing rope, or like other horses that, tragically, have jumped off cliffs, knocked over people, and raced across busy highways, all because they were not taught to accept a dropped rein.

Cold or hot, wet or dry, school was in: these were not fair-weather lessons. When it rained, we worked on ground cues inside the barn. Lucy was a fast learner, backing up with a wave of my hand towards her chest and moving away from pressure if I nudged her in the shoulders or along her flank. In winter, when snow drifted along the lane, I attached driving lines to her halter, jogging along behind as if my feet were sled runners. Sometimes I put a collar of jingle bells around her neck, just so I could listen to the merry sound and pretend I was driving a one-mule open sleigh.

During these sessions, Mom often leaned against the fence or sat on a hill, watching the two of us match wits. Some days it was tough to tell who was winning, she said, as the two redheads jockeyed to be boss. Many times she said her life was repeating itself, as she recalled watching my dad train horses. Long before my time, they too owned horses—a fiery mustang called Judy and a palomino named Tootsie. Later came Penny, a lovely red mare and retired racehorse that they harnessed to a cutter, a light two-seater sleigh. The horses, of course, are long gone, but their memories have travelled here, their bits and breast collars, hand-tooled by my father, hanging in our mud room.

When Lucy turned three, I started to talk about climbing aboard her broad back, an event none of the neighbours wanted to miss, especially Pete. "Hear those mules can really buck," he said. "I'd like to come by and see that." Others wondered if the big show would ever happen, or if Lucy and I were professional students, having fun but with no intention of putting our lessons into practice. "Got that mule broke yet?" Bill, a close neighbour, called out one day as he rode by. A former rodeo champ, Bill is all business when it comes to horses. You won't find a bag of sugar cubes in his barn.

"Not quite," I said. "But we're getting there, slow and

easy." Bill frowned, then smiled, and kept on riding. He knew there was some big-time spoiling going on and that, in his hands, Lucy would be playing Trigger by now. But I was paranoid about making mistakes, about rushing her too fast. Compared to horses, mules are about a year behind in mental and physical development. Push them too hard and they sour, losing their willingness to work.

I must have heaved the saddle on and off Lucy's back at least a dozen times before I finally left it there, easing up the cinch and double-checking that it wasn't pinching or grabbing any hair. And when it came to a bit: well, she carried that snaffle around for three days until she stopped trying to paw it off or grind it into the dirt and grass.

As the big day approached, I began slipping one foot into the stirrup, while keeping my other foot on the ground. With a hank of Lucy's mane in one hand, I would haul myself up so she could feel the weight. One day, probably bored with the routine, she let me pull her off-balance, my hand on the saddle horn as she crumpled her legs, dropping her body onto my foot like a dog lying at my feet. I might not have been riding her yet, but I could already make her lie down. Maybe I too could train her to be the next Trigger.

Few have planned a first ride like I planned mine. I knew Lucy was ready, and I had long ago run out of excuses as to why I wasn't. I had read every mule-training book and attended several horsemanship clinics, including one with the legendary Ray Hunt, a man who thinks like a horse and teaches harmony between a horse and its rider. I even took two weeks of riding lessons, just to get back into the rhythm. Yes, it was definitely time to get in the saddle. So one night, I listened to the weather. The next day promised plenty of sun and no wind. Perfect. I lay in bed, visualizing sitting square on Lucy's back, dreaming we were riding together like two ol' sodbusters. I hoped she was having the same dream.

The next day, after saddling Lucy in the round pen, I called Mom to come watch. I wanted her to be part of the big event, but I also wanted somebody around to call an ambulance if need be. I put my foot in the stirrup, grabbed a piece of Lucy's mane, and then slowly swung my leg over her back. I paused for two seconds, easing myself down into the saddle. My stomach was in a knot, but I made myself breathe. In and out, in and out.

"What is she doing?" I said to Mom, who was holding the lead close to the halter.

"Well, her eyes are huge, sort of rolling in the back of her head. But other than that, she seems fine."

I told Mom to step to the side and let Lucy go.

"If she bucks, or goes nuts, just get out of the way."

"What will you do?" Mom asked.

"I don't know. I haven't thought about it yet," I said.

So here we were, just Lucy and I. For three years, we had worked together, always with this day in mind. Now she was about to let me know what she thought of me. Lucy stood still, as if her hooves were nailed to the ground. Her head didn't flinch, her tail didn't swish, and I could barely feel her breathing. Only her ears danced, one tipped forward and the other back; then they would trade places. I squeezed with my legs and clucked to her.

"Walk on, Lucy," I said, but she didn't move. I squeezed harder and clucked louder. "Walk on, Lucy." Nothing.

I asked Mom to lead her around, just like she did when I was five years old and riding my first pony at a fair at the local shopping plaza. Lucy took a step forward, then froze again. Then another step. She was trying to find her balance, like someone after an all-night binge trying to walk a straight line. Slowly, she put the steps together and we shuffled around the pen, completing one whole circle. I wanted to scream, to yell to the world to see me on my mule that I'd trained myself. We may not have been the most dazzling couple, but I felt like royalty, as if I were riding a white Lipizzaner stallion. There never was a miniature Calgary Stampede bucking show, at least not that day. And the neighbours never did drop by to hoot and holler and pick up the pummelled pieces. There was just Lucy, Mom, and I. And I like to think that there was one other person leaning over the fence, that my dad was there cheering me on, proud to know another Dudley was about to ride the range.

Chapter Twenty-Three

Two Broads and a Mule

No wonder Mom and I are attracted to donkeys and mules. We're beasts of burden ourselves!

I scowled at the truck's flat tire, its sides bulging like a pancaked mud pie and a fat nail so deeply embedded in it that only its round head was visible.

"You know what this means, don't you?" I said to Mom, both of us dirty and weary from loading and hauling three truckloads of baled hay. "We're going to have to unload all these bales, then wait for the guy to fix the tire, and then go back for the last load. So if we're going to make it into town for dinner, we're going to have to take a change of clothes with us and drive straight to town."

Mom nodded in agreement, the two of us aware of the darkening sky to the west. Racing the storm clouds, we tossed the bales from the back of the truck, keeping our thoughts to ourselves. I wondered why we were always in a rush and why everything goes wrong when we can least afford it to go wrong. And why do we always promise my brother, who lives in the city, that we'll be there in time for the family dinner? The questions flowed like a funnel of grain, but I had no answers.

Settling into our plough-horse pace, Mom and I swung the bales into a wheelbarrow, then pushed the loads across the paddock and into the barn. We dumped the bales on the ground and wrestled them through the narrow stall-room door, whose width shrinks every year, I am sure. Then we stacked the sixty-pound brutes from the floor to the rafters, keeping them far enough back from the stall bars that Lucy couldn't stretch her rubbery lips and steal a mouthful. With my apologies to the porcine species, it is a "pig" of a job, sweaty, dusty, and itchy. I feel like a pincushion by the end of the day. Prickly hay stalks slip down my pants, under my collar, and through my socks, while alfalfa leaves find their way to the most unusual places. When we pause for a rare break, Mom and I cough and hack up black dirt and dust—a mild and temporary case of farmer's lung.

Leaning against the tailgate, I asked a question.

"So, did you expect to be stacking hay bales in your lifetime?"

"Can't say I did," Mom said, her fitness masking her near eighty years. Heaving another bale from the truck, she yelled, "Come on. We better get this hay unloaded before that man arrives to fix the tire." I guess there are some things not worthy of deep conversation, and this was one of them.

Mom and I have never been afraid of using our arms and backs, but we don't necessarily work well together, pecking away at one another like two crusty ol' hens. But by the end of the day, the chores are done and we're still on speaking terms, which, for most mothers and daughters, is quite an achievement. My mother's friends say they could never live with their daughters; my friends say they could never live with their mothers. It's sad, because the memories you make as adults are so different from those you make as parent and child. People raise their eyebrows when they hear that Mom and I live under the same roof, but it wasn't that many years ago when parents, children, in-laws, and grandchildren worked the same piece of land. Look at Hoss, Adam, and Little Joe. They lived with Pa Cartwright at the Ponderosa. And what about John Boy Walton and his siblings? They sat around the dinner table every night with Grandma and Grandpa, and I don't remember anyone thinking them strange. Even today, many ranching families live next door to one another, sharing machinery and muscle, good years and bad. My friend's grandfather worked the farm with his son and grandson until he died a few months short of his hundredth birthday. Living in a small house across the yard, he was always within shouting distance of the back kitchen door.

Now, I'd be the first to admit that Mom and I go squirrelly from time to time, nattering away over something as small as a pine nut. Like housekeeping: my cleaning may not be up to snuff in my mother's eyes, but what daughter's is? She'll never understand a writer's habit of saving every scrap of paper, every newspaper clipping and magazine article that may someday come in handy as background information. Or maybe it's the way I store these valuables that drives her crazy. Yes, I have a filing system. It's called organized chaos. My office floor is covered with papers, making my room look like a dog kennel, one that's in danger of spreading into my bedroom, as well as the dining room, living room, and laundry room. But hey, I know where everything is, so don't mess with it. Besides, I have to put up with my mother's orderliness: tea towels folded a certain way, dish cloths left to dry a certain way, this utensil in that drawer, that utensil in this drawer, and heaven forbid if you mix them up.

It's enough to make you laugh, and on most days we do. A healthy sense of humour will cure most of life's headaches. A touch of whimsy also helps, so we recently hung from our gate a wooden cut-out of two blackbirds perched above the words Two Old Crows Live Here.

I sometimes refer to our set-up as "Two Broads and a Mule." Neighbours are kinder, addressing us (at least to our faces) as "the ladies" or "the gals." Others, quite accurately, think of us as hermits. It's not that we're anti-social, but with so much work to do, we have little time for meeting over cups of coffee. Most of our catching up is done over the gate or down at the general store. In some ways, I can't blame people for scratching their heads. We live in a swampy hollow, with a guard mule and donkey, and, before it was stolen, we had a bear skull wired to the front gate, its canines greeting all incoming visitors. Perched on the rails is a silhouetted murder of black crows, their metal bodies often mocking hordes of ravens, a scavenging bird attracted to death. All of this had a television producer, who arrived to shoot a segment on unusual pets, creeping down our lane until I met him halfway. Slowly rolling down his window, he looked more than a little nervous.

"I was just asking the cameraman whether he thought you'd come out with a shotgun or something. I wasn't too sure what to expect," he said.

OK, maybe the fence needed a paint job, but I didn't think the place looked like Hillbilly Hollow. Why is it that people who own mules are suspected of running illegal stills and holing up like criminals on the run?

Taking advantage of the situation, I decided to have some fun.

"Actually, the shotgun's back at the house, up against the porch wall, behind the rocking chair, next to the banjo," I said, eventually cracking a smile so the poor fellow knew I was kidding.

I guess what baffles people is that we do most of the work ourselves, without machinery and without a hired hand. But believe me, with my mom's back of bronze, a hired hand would get in the way. She swings a mean axe, hammers a straight nail, and gives a cold eye that could freeze a bear in its tracks. Between the two of us, we shovel a snowbound laneway that measures about two football fields and we clear trails and cut our wood without a chainsaw, preferring a cross-blade or bow saw. My riding trails are pruned with lopping shears, the paths just wide enough for the mule's fat belly and my stubby legs, with bruised knees a regular mishap. We spread and rake our manure by hand, cut hay with a scythe, take down fences, put up fences, hand-pull weeds, haul rocks from the creek (sometimes we cheat and use the donkey to pack them out), and sleep in the barn with sick animals. Much of this is because the cabin where we once lived on weekends and holidays had no power, heat, or running water, so if you didn't want to freeze, starve, or die of thirst, you learned to use your backbone. Another reason I shun most machinery is that I am not mechanically inclined, and get easily frustrated when a turn of the key fails to fire up the engine. I look at a motor and it stalls. And Mom, well, she doesn't even drive.

We prefer the primitive look, fortunately, because much of what we patch and build is far from pretty.

Take the first gate I hung, a job that just about gave me a hernia. First, the posthole I dug hit about four inches of water. But if the post was to line up with the existing fence, it had to go there, so I kept pouring dirt down the hole, hoping the clay would set up like concrete. It didn't. Next, I tried drilling holes for the gate bolts, but the bit was too short to screw through the post to the other side, so I had to drill two holes, hoping they would match up. Of course, they didn't. By chipping and banging and turning the air blue, I eventually hung that monster steel gate, but I almost twisted my intestines straining to lift it off the ground.

"You're going to ruin your insides, you know," my mom said, watching me groan under the dead weight. "Women aren't supposed to do this kind of work." I laughed.

"Well, I don't see any guy standing here, so who do you think is going to do it?" I said, ending the conversation on an abrupt note. That gate is still there, but it drags across the ground, digging a channel of mud in the spring, and ploughing a windrow of snow in winter. Someday I'll fix it, but not today, and probably not tomorrow.

Some neighbours think we're as stubborn as the mules and donkeys we care for, knowing we'll never ask for help unless it's an emergency, but we prefer to call it old-fashioned pride. We didn't move out here expecting people to drop everything to help two ol' gals down the road. When we can no longer lift a bale or dig a hole, we'll know it's time to move on. When we do, we'll know we cared for our land, leaving it a better place than when we arrived. Anyway, we never really own land; we just borrow it. In the meantime, we're weaving some wonderful memories to take with us: meadow mornings when everything is fresh with new sunlight; sailing through a sea of grass, with the dogs riding the crests and Hud the cat tiptoeing behind; watching geese fly overhead, their wings catching a piece of autumn grey sky; sipping morning coffee on the back deck as the butterflies float above the summer garden; seeing falling stars streak across a black sky; listening to the crows call our name; turning the mule and donkeys out each morning, the dew shining their hooves; and sitting by the fire at night, calling it a day, while outside the northern lights splash waves of red and green. These are the moments that will be tucked inside our journals, precious and private moments shared between a mother and a daughter.

Chapter Twenty-Four

Fergus

Fergus, my orange cat, is missing. I last saw him this morning when he wandered outside, straying to the top of the hill where he sometimes likes to nibble grass. With friends and family dropping by for a visit, I forgot to check on him, only noticing his absence at dinnertime when he didn't show up for his meal. Mom and I combed the house, opening cupboards, peeking under beds, and even checking the clothes dryer. Searching among the tools in the outside shed and the stacked boxes inside the open garage, we called his name over and over, but there was no answer. I even let blind Hud tag along, thinking his mewing might bring Fergus out of hiding.

This is so out of character for Fergus. A fearful cat, he rarely strays, considering a journey of twenty feet beyond the house a wild adventure. Normally, when we know he is outside, we keep the sliding door open so he can flee indoors, but today there was no passage to safety, leaving him at the mercy of the barking dogs and a savage afternoon thunderstorm. Poor Fergus, he'd be frantic, his hair bristled and his pathetic little mew a mere whisper among the clashing clouds and reckless wind.

With forty-five acres, you don't know where to start looking for a cat, especially one that trembles when a patch of dry orchard grass rustles, a dog yips, or a raven croaks. Neither worldly nor smart, Fergus's chances of surviving

Dog people are often not cat people, but I enjoy the company of both animals. During the day, I love the shameless loyalty of a dog, but at night, I am drawn to the soothing purr of a cat curled in my lap.

a night outside are slim. Orange cats camouflage well in the desert, but out here they're like lighthouses against a sea of green grass. Of the feral barn cats we've owned, the pumpkin ones disappear first, grabbed by hawks, owls, coyotes, or weasels.

It's dark now, and we've left the windows and screen doors open, just in case he comes home during the night, scratching and mewing with the hope we will hear him. Already I miss his chirping meow, his warm body curled up next to my toes, his gentle pat-pat on my face, and his favourite game of batting moths. I find the empty space in the house cruel, as I stare at the loft above my bed where he sits for hours in what I call his treehouse, content to study life below. I want to leave candles burning in the window, like a guiding light to welcome him home; I must hope, I can't give up, but guilt seeps in as I start to think of Fergus in the past tense.

He was just a teacup-sized kitten when I found him at a farmers' market, so sweet and cuddly, with hair the colour of beach sand. As the months went by, he bonded with Hud, my teddy bear of a brown tabby, kneading his ample belly while snuggled close to his chest. The two played crazy nocturnal cat games, bounding through the house and up and over the furniture, as if the chairs and sofas were trees in a jungle. Hud became his king, while I was relegated to being caterer and water girl, except when it came to baths. Whenever I soaked in the tub, Fergus would walk along the edge, yowling until I dribbled handfuls of warm, soapy water along his spine. He'd arch his back, flick his tail and rev up his purring, never satisfied until he was dripping water from his ginger tail to his pink triangle of a nose. Outside the bathroom, however, I was often the victim of what I can only call a nasty streak. If I lay in bed, he pounced on my belly, and in the morning he batted my eyelids, using his claws if I refused to get up. And I can't say he held onto his cute looks, since, as an adult, he was cow-hocked and missing a few teeth. But he wasn't unhealthy, having rung up a vet bill only once in his eleven years, when he stuffed himself with his own hair. He finally threw up the wad, a hairball the size of a baseball. Quirks and all, I loved him, embracing him, as I do all the animals that come to stay at Burro Alley.

This is ridiculous; I must stop thinking of Fergus as gone, as an animal I once owned. He could still come home. I must remain positive.

In the night, I dream of him, waking because I'm sure I hear his plaintive call. I get up earlier than usual, looking out all the windows and checking the decks and the doorsteps, but he isn't there. When I let the dogs out, Maggie runs into the garage whining, but she doesn't dive into the corner piled high with boxes and books the way she does if a squirrel or barn cat is hiding. Back in the kitchen, I make the animals' breakfast, filling two bowls with tinned food and a sprinkle of dry crunch. Fergus's dish sits empty. I have had pets die before, so I know the stages of grief and recovery, the dreams, the phantom mews, and finally the letting go, but still, I hate this. Struggling to accept his possible death, I recall having read somewhere that wild animals go numb moments before they are attacked, and that their souls leave their bodies seconds before death strikes. I cling to this, clutching it as I would a rope pulling me to safety. Animals have souls—they must, because a heaven without them would indeed be a lonely place.

After breakfast, Mom and I walk through the bush,

looking for tufts of yellow hair, remnants that will at least bring closure. Otherwise, I will forever scan fields for a streak of familiar orange. Finding nothing, I am miserable.

It is late afternoon and I'm sitting outside with a book and a mug of tea. I hear a mew and Hud, who's lying next to me, raises his head. Then silence. I shrug it off as another phantom voice. Then another mew. The dogs stop playing, their ears perked. My heart flutters. Around the corner of the house steps Fergus. I want to jump up, run over, sweep him into my arms, and smother him with kisses, but he darts into the house, a blur of yellow. I run inside, yelling to Mom that Fergus is home, that the cat has come back. We rejoice, hugging the dogs and cooing to this waif of a ginger cat. That night, while I'm filling the tub, in parades Fergus, eager for his bubble bath. He purrs as I sponge his face, then sits and stares at me the way cats do. I tickle his ears and whisper how much I love him. Heaven will have to wait.

Fearless Farriers

After three weeks and dozens of phone calls, I was still trying to find someone willing to trim mule and donkey hooves. One farrier was polite enough to respond, even if he did say he wouldn't touch anything called *Equus asinus*, but most just ignored my desperate phone messages. Horses too can have nasty tantrums over their pedicures, but donkeys and mules are blacklisted before anyone touches their feet, receiving a guilty verdict without a chance to prove their innocence.

Now four months old, Lucy was ready for her first trim. I handled her feet almost every day, tapping her hooves so she wouldn't be alarmed when the farrier rasped and filed her toes. At first, wide-eyed and twitching, she would jerk her leg, but I held on, not letting go until she settled down. If she behaved, I released her leg, so she soon learned that standing still has its rewards. But convincing potential farriers that she was indeed a good girl, though cheeky at times, was another matter. Stories about how I could pick stones from her hooves without risking my life were considered fables. By the time I contacted Steve Bennett, a farrier used by some of my neighbours, I was suffering from repeated rejection. Before he even answered, I gave him an out.

"You might not want to come," I said. " I just have the donkey and mule. And there's only a single light bulb in the barn, and it isn't heated. And you should know that the mule is young, so this would be her first trim. So I don't know how you feel about this. If you think it's too much of a bother, that's OK."

Several times the poor man tried to interrupt, but he couldn't plug my pessimism. I must have sounded like Eeyore, so gloomy and grey-dayish.

"It's OK," he said. "I'll come."

"Really? You will? Oh, that's wonderful. She's a pretty little mule, and I've done some work with her, so maybe she won't be that bad," I said, my spirits lifting like a thinning slate cloud just before the sun comes out.

But Steve didn't need convincing. A long-time solid-as-a-rock mule man, he's one of the best when it comes to understanding their unique ways. For years, he worked with mules in the outfitting business, where their sure-footedness and gentle walk make them the preferred pack animal. Because they move forward instead of rocking from side to side like a horse, their loads are more likely to remain balanced in rugged terrain, a bonus when you're riding in the backcountry and can't afford to lose half your goods along the trail.

It was almost dark, with a light snow falling, when Steve arrived at the front door. Immediately I knew he was the right one for my Lucy. A genuine horseman, he looked like he'd walked off the pages of a Will James story, his long legs built to wrap around the barrel of a tall horse and his hands strong and scarred from a life spent working with hooves and nails. A dark felt hat shadowed his brow and a loosely tied bandana collared his neck.

Moving slowly, he spoke softly, shrugging off my worries like a seasoned pack horse. Nothing was a problem; not the snow, the ice, the cold, or the pale light.

I was still apologizing for my primitive set-up when we arrived at the barn, but he never said a word, his eyes searching the paddock for the mule.

"Here she comes," I said, as Lucy trotted around the corner. Spotting Steve, she dug in her hooves. A new person, new smells—a stranger. Steve spoke quietly, letting her come to him. He smelled good, like horses, like her mare mother.

"That's a good girl," I whispered, as Steve picked up her front foot, picking out the mud from around the frog at the centre of the hoof. It wasn't until he started to trim that she began to fray like the loose end of a string. She tried yanking her leg away, but Steve held on. The two of them see-sawed back and forth, Lucy tugging his arm and Steve giving and taking with each pull. When Lucy didn't get her way, she gave up.

Discipline should not be part of a farrier's job, but Steve's a natural with horses, having spent five years as a trainer on the Ya Ha Tinda Ranch, the home base for horses used in western Canada's national parks. He developed his passion young, sketching horses in the margins of his school notebooks and using the money he saved from his paper route to buy an Arabian cross. She was barely broke, but he rode her the ten miles home. Being only fifteen, he did not yet own a trailer.

Lucy may not have been as big as the horses he was used to training, but by the time he finished trimming her hooves, she had reared, kicked the barn wall, and stepped not on his foot, but on mine. Just another youngster enduring growing pains, Steve said.

"She really wasn't all that bad, considering it was her first trim," he added. "Just keep handling her lots." I took this to mean he would come again, and that I could stop apologizing.

Lucy did indeed improve, but not without trying to master a bag of evasive tricks. She would stretch her neck forward, then rotate it sideways as she lowered her head to the ground, twisting my arm as I tried to hold on. Turning around to see Steve still working on her hind leg, she would then flop down, her tail thumping and sweeping the ground like a dog's. Her favourite joke, however, was the leaning game: pushing against Steve until he had to fight to keep his balance while he tried to cradle one of her hooves between his legs. Accepting only so much abuse, he would eventually elbow her in the ribs.

After several such pranks, I decided Lucy was due for a lesson. What might be amusing in a young animal isn't so funny once the animal weighs a thousand pounds. So Steve and I plotted a plan that worked wonders. The next time Lucy shifted her weight, Steve gave me the nod, a sign that I was to let her go. Dropping her lead, I stepped back, as did Steve. Without her private leaning post, she collapsed to the ground, with a thud and a look of disbelief. We hadn't touched her: it was as if she had tripped herself. After a few grunts and groans, she got up. She stood there still as a heron, her weight evenly planted on three legs while Steve finished each foot. She never leaned again.

It's been nine years since Steve first drove his truck down the lane to Burro Alley. Lucy adores him, nickering when he pulls in and nipping his jacket collar when he gives her a pat. She slimes his chaps and tugs at the hoof pick in his back pocket, excited at his return after six to eight weeks. He's always on time, and he appreciates the difference between a mule hoof and a horse hoof, the angles on a mule's being more upright than in a horse. A mule or donkey with improperly trimmed hooves can easily go lame. It's a common ailment, as many people neglect their animals, allowing their feet to grow so long they turn up like elf shoes.

Because I don't ride my animals on hard surfaces, I allow them to go without shoes, making Steve's stop at my place pretty straightforward, but still, it's a thankless job, leaning over all day like a tree bent in a strong westerly. There are moody mares, cranky owners, and, in spring, mudholes up to mid-calf. And so much can go wrong: a horse that spooks can drive a shoeing nail into your hand; a fractious animal may break your arm or crack your rib, sidelining you for months. When Steve inquired about insurance, he was told he would be ranked the same as a stuntman.

Lucy and I know that someday Steve will hang up his farrier tools, though I don't think he will ever pack away his chaps and saddle. A cowboy through and through, he may once again hit the rugged trails, working from the back of a horse instead of from behind it. But it will take a team of horses—or perhaps I should say a mile-long mule train—to keep Lucy from seeing her favourite farrier. When the day comes, Lucy and I will track him down, hoping for just one more pedicure.

Chapter Twenty-Six

When I walk through the forest, my eyes search for cougars. When I walk through the desert, I look and listen for rattlesnakes. Nature teaches us to stay on our toes.

Where Cougars Walk

I placed my hand in the mitten-sized paw print. Even with my fingers stretched, the tips were still a good half inch short of reaching the track's outer edge. I climbed back up on Lucy and we continued across the snow-laden meadow, my eyes darting from bush to tree to bush. Lucy's gait was choppy, her head was high, her ears pointed, and her eyes open wide. Resting one hand on her mane, just in front of the saddle horn, I tried to calm her, but those tracks were as clear as a blue winter sky—massive paws with a heart-shaped pad, set out in a single line. A cougar, a big one, probably a male hunting alone.

Cougars are solitary and curious, not unlike sofa-loving cats, but it bothered me to think a pair of pale yellow eyes was watching from somewhere in the snowdrifts. Even though I knew our creek valley was a natural corridor for the big cats, there seemed to be more sightings than usual this year, many in broad daylight. Several horses, sheep, pigs, and pet dogs had been killed, their remains often raked and left under a mound of leaves and dirt. The deer, who usually criss-cross our meadows by the dozens, had moved out.

Squeezing my legs lightly, I pressed the saddle's fender against Lucy's sides, the leather creaking in the cold like a rusty door hinge. With the snow now flying horizontally, I had to squint to see the trail ahead. Suddenly the cat's tracks changed from individual prints to wallows, big gouges in the snow from where the cougar had begun to bound downhill, until the depressions disappeared beneath the low-lying boughs of a giant spruce, its skirt less than a foot from the trail we were travelling. With the wind now tossing the snow every which way, deafening all other sounds and scattering wild scents, I pulled Lucy in. She was willing to stop, but not for long, sensing this was not a good place to be. I heeled her left flank and we turned in a tight circle, heading east and home.

The two of us lowered our heads, both our manes now knotted by the wind. Every few seconds, I glanced over my shoulder, just to make sure we weren't being followed, but with our decision to head for the barn, Lucy was now relaxed and I trusted her instincts. I urged her into a trot, relieved when we broke trail down the last hill, the sides of the red barn now visible through the grey aspens. Slipping off Lucy's saddle, I rubbed her back dry and then gave her a flake of hay before turning her loose with the donkey. Heading back to the house, I noticed her hoofprints already vanishing under the swirling snow.

"Cougar's around," I said to Mom, who was preparing dinner at the stove.

"We'll have to keep an eye on Lucy and Raven, maybe keep them up by the barn at night."

Within a few hours, the storm had blown itself out, the clouds now brushing the plains of Saskatchewan. I made a quick trip to the barn, forking the hay into two mounds in the paddock. Hearing Lucy and Raven leave their shed, their hooves squeaking and crunching over the cold snow, I waited until they arrived.

"You two take care of each other now. No sleeping at the same time," I whispered, patting each one on the neck before bidding them a safe night. Back in the house, I stacked my pillows, snuggled between my flannelette sheets, and began to read. Within minutes, the outdoor sensor light went on. I knew it was too cold for the barn cat to be prowling about and too still for it to be a wind-whipped tree, so maybe the deer were heading up the hill to lick clean the bird feeders. Sitting up and leaning towards the window, I studied the snowdrifts, their troughs and crests flooded by light, but there was no sign of movement. Then, pressing my nose against the window, I looked down to our back deck. At first, I wasn't sure if what I was seeing was real, but I couldn't mistake those yellow eyes staring back. The cougar didn't move, just stood on the deck, studying my face in the window. His round amber eyes penetrated my soul, and I was paralyzed by his beauty; he had a long back smooth with sleek muscle, powerful furred feet, a sweeping golden tail, and a stunning, intelligent face with a snow-white muzzle and a black moustache. His entire being was magnificent, a perfect specimen of grace and power. I was hypnotized by his stare, my feet frozen to the floor. I wanted to get my camera, but I couldn't move. I was afraid this was a winter mirage that would soon melt into the night. Slowly, very slowly, the cougar began to back up, one foot at a time, placing each foot in the track behind. It would be a trail with an abrupt end, one without a set of retreating prints. Not until he slipped into the blackness did I realize I had been holding my breath.

This was my first glimpse of a wild cougar, and it left my heart pounding and my lungs pleading for air. Awakening from my trance, I remembered Lucy and Raven, feeding on their hay only strides away from where the cougar was headed. Hesitant to venture outside, I opened the front door and then slammed it shut, hoping the heavy bang might sound like a warning gunshot. Other than that, the girls were on their own. I feared for their safety, but country living comes with risks, and this was one of them.

Several weeks later, a photograph of a hunter kneeling over a dead cougar appeared in the regional newspaper. Apparently the cat had attacked and killed a miniature horse. Reading about his impressive size, I sensed it was the same cougar I had watched from my window. It saddened me to know he was gone, but I also understood the loss of livestock. Once the cougar discovered that killing penned animals was easier than chasing fleeing deer, he could become an opportunistic feeder, preferring to raid horse and sheep pens than to hunt in the wild.

With the community growing nervous, a cougar expert was brought in to explain the cat's behaviour and to give a balanced perspective. Yes, cougar sightings were on the increase, but only because there were more people living in their foothills habitat, an area that happens to have one of the continent's highest cougar densities. We were told that there are fewer than four cougar attacks a year in North America, compared to a whopping 220,000 dog attacks. Personally, I have suffered dog bites three times, but I've never been chomped by a cougar! I was told that, if I were to encounter a cougar, I should make myself appear larger than life by waving a stick in the air and jumping up and down while hooting and hollering. Such a commotion might convince the cat that I was a predator and scare it off. I've also been told that stitching cut-outs of eyes to the back of a hat may deter a cougar attack. Better yet is donning a Hallowe'en mask backwards, as hunters in Asia do when hiking in tiger territory. Now, that would be something for the local gossip circle—Mom and I making our daily walks as two-faced ghouls!

While cougars are built to kill, they too have their

problems. Without much of a fight, they will give up their carcasses to wolves and bears. And then, of course, there's us. People. We move into their territory, then clear brush from our fields and leave trees around our house, creating a cougar corridor outside our front doors. As development pushes the big cats into marginal areas where there are no moose, elk, or deer—their favourite prey—they resort to killing pets and livestock, often slaughtering an entire pen of sheep. A cougar will usually kill and consume one animal, but domestic goats and sheep appear to be the exception. Several neighbours have awakened to a pen of corpses; panicking sheep tend to huddle together, and this may confuse the cougar, triggering a furious rampage. Sheep ranchers living in cougar country often use livestock protection dogs, especially the Akbash, a breed known for its speed, aggression, and unwillingness to back down from cougars, bears, or wolves.

Most attending the meeting left with less fear, realizing they were at a greater risk of being bitten by the neighbour's dog than of being attacked by a cougar. But there were some who suggested that the only good cougar is a dead cougar, and that conservation officials should consider eradicating them. At one point, it looked like we were headed for a resurrection of the historic range wars, when cattlemen and sheep farmers were at odds over land and water. Said one rancher, "I'll tell you what the problem is. It's all the sheep out here. They don't belong. This is cattle country."

Several years have passed since that winter when so many cougars roamed our valley. I see their winter tracks, so I know they are still here, but the deer have returned and sheep are grazing next to fields speckled with cattle. If only we could get people to live peacefully next to one another, and accept that the wilderness and its predators are part of the beauty we wake to each day.

Chapter Twenty-Seven

Cowboy Trail

We are not ranchers, nor are we farmers. Mom and I do not put food on our table by growing grain or selling cattle, horses, chickens, pigs, or sheep—or anything else that eats while we sleep. As for the donkeys, my attempts to breed them have so far been humorous, if not downright pathetic.

What brought me to the country was my love of open spaces, wilderness, and Old West culture. I like wrapping myself in a quiet evening, taking in the baritones of bellowing cattle and the smell of sweet hay and aging manure, and then falling asleep under a sea of stars, drifting with the likes of Roy Rogers and Will James down some dreamland cattle trail. I like waking up to a rose-coloured morning and seeing my posse of longears traipsing across the fields, their wispy tails fanning their rumps. But none of this makes me a lariat-swinging cowgirl—an armchair wrangler perhaps, but not a woman who makes her living from sowing seeds, herding cows, and viewing the world from the back of a horse.

I like to think, however, that through my writing I have left a welcome hoofprint in cow country, an invisible signature posted along one of Alberta's most scenic stretches of highway, known as the Cowboy Trail. In writing a newspaper story about the tourism project, I suggested it be called the "trail of the cowboy."

Wouldn't it be grand to retrace some of those old cowboy trails? Years ago, I met an innkeeper who re-rode the Sante Fe Trail. He said it changed his life.

Little did I know that the name would stick like flies to honey sauce, and that a year or two later dozens of red and black Cowboy Trail signs, emblazoned with a silhouette of a horse and rider, would be posted along Highways 5, 6, and 22. Approximately 420 miles long, the foothills route follows a corridor of heritage ranchlands from Cardston, near southern Alberta's Waterton Lakes National Park, to Mayerthorpe, northwest of Edmonton. Along the way are some wonderful Wild West ranch names, such as the Lazy M, Ride the Wind, Spirit Walker, Willow Lane, Homeplace, and Mount Sentinel Diamond Willow Beef. Driving past the Cowboy Trail signs, I remind myself that I want a friend to take a photograph of me leaning against one before they are all stolen. Several go missing each year, no doubt taken as a western souvenir to hang above someone's basement pool table.

When the Cowboy Trail project won a provincial tourism award for innovative marketing, I was invited to attend the ceremony by my friend Rob Miller, then a tourism marketing director for the Calgary area. It was a gesture of thanks for providing the name, he said. I rode tall in the saddle that night, but of course the real heroes are the men and women still working the ranges. Without them, there would be no Cowboy Trail.

But I confess I'm rather proud of my contribution to cowboy history, since it's about as close as I'll ever get to the Cowboy Hall of Fame. After all, I can't throw the Houlihan, I can't ride a bronc (though as a colt, Lucy sure knew how to round her back for more than eight seconds), I've never butchered my own beef, and I don't even own a horse trailer. I don't have a gun rack in my pickup, and my best field crop is purple thistle.

I say all this because if there's one thing I've learned, it's never to pass yourself off as something you're not. Rural folk can smell a ripe tale the minute they spot your car coming up the lane, and if the jalopy doesn't give you away, what happens once you step outside the car will.

I've been bitten by ranch dogs and bluff-charged by bulls. Worse yet, I've sat like the village idiot behind the steering wheel of my teensy-weensy car while a rancher fired up his tractor to haul me up his steep lane—not once, but twice. The first time was when I was caught in his coulee during a blizzard, my car not even making it to the first bend in the lane. Two weeks later I visited the same rancher. The snow was gone, but his road was now a speed skater's delight. Out came the tractor and chains, and my promise to stay away until summer.

I guess I could drive a four-wheel drive like most of my neighbours, but writing from home doesn't exactly leave my banker wanting to hand over a hefty loan. There's my second-hand, trusty and rusty pickup, but it's only rear-wheel drive. Unless it's packed with firewood or wet hay bales, it flops all over the road like a fish out of water.

Such incidents are embarrassing, like the time I walked backwards while trying to take a picture of a horse-drawn wagon, unaware of the wallow in the deep grass. With no warning from the wagon master, I stepped into the hole, toppling over, feet up in the air, with only the camera visible above the tall grass as I struggled to hold it away from my body. Trying to make light of the moment, I laughed at my awkwardness, but the two wagonmen just sat and stared from their high perches. Not a crack of a smile to be seen for a mile.

Now, I'm the first to admit that I don't know a lot about cows, though I do know a heifer from a steer and a Holstein from a Hereford, but I don't read them well. So I guess it was only a matter of time before I landed in trouble while tagging along on foot beside a cattle drive. Coincidentally, we were moving them along a portion of the Cowboy Trail. Everything was going fine until I circled around out front to take a picture. When the herd came to a standstill, I figured the cattle were just pausing for a quick graze.

"Get out of there, you xx?!@#*!" I heard the trail boss yell. But the herd didn't budge. A rider then approached. "Better move along, you're spooking the herd," he said.

"I thought he was hollering at the cows," I replied. "Nope," he answered. "Cows are OK. You're not."

I quickly saddled my metal war pony, Toyota Jane, and hit the blacktop, watching the riders and cattle vanish in my rear-view mirror. Fortunately, as the brochures say, you don't need a horse or cow to travel the Cowboy Trail.

Chapter Twenty-Eight

Midnight Colic

I snapped the driving whip against Lucy's buttocks, pleading with her to "get up, get up," but she didn't flinch. She was stretched out in the short-cropped grass, her eyes closed, her lips curled back, and her teeth clenched. The hair from above her bony brow was gone. With each spasm of pain in her belly, she would grind her head into the ground, tearing out tufts of hair. Usually we can walk Lucy out of colic, a bellyache often caused by an impacted intestine or buildup of gas, but five hours had passed since we found her lying in the shade of a spruce tree, the grass flattened from where she had been rolling in an attempt to relieve the painful symptoms. A stomach ache may not sound like such a big deal, but equine colic can be fatal if the animal twists its intestine by thrashing and rolling. Big Ben, the champion Canadian show jumping horse owned by Olympic equestrian Ian Miller, was a colicky horse, succumbing to the ailment in 1999. Everything from bad feed, to change of feed, to too little water can bring on a colic attack.

In Lucy's case, I suspect it has to do with lack of water. She's a sipper, preferring to swish the water with her lips, stick her tongue in it, swill it around in her mouth, and only if she remembers, actually swallow a mouthful or two. She used to be a bed-eater, the straw and shavings absorbing what little moisture she took in. When we

I envy those who grew up on farms, accepting death as easily as birth. As I have been told many times: "If you've got livestock, you're going to have dead stock. It's a fact of life."

removed her bedding, the colic stopped. We thought we had it beat, but here we were, two years later, with her worst bout ever.

We waited several hours before calling the horse doctor because, frankly, Lucy is a true redhead, a bit of a "drama queen," as one vet described her. One little gas bubble and she crumples to the ground, yet all she has to do is pass one puff of flatulence and she's right back to her amusing self. There's nothing more frustrating—or expensive—than calling the vet only to have the patient standing bright-eyed when help arrives. But this time, nothing seemed to relieve Lucy's symptoms. We walked her until our soles began to thin, we sat on her sides massaging her belly until our arms ached, and we syringed several grams of phenylbutazone, a painkiller paste, into the sides of her mouth. When she would no longer get up off the ground, we knew it was time to call the vet.

Lucy loves horses—after all, her mother was a horse—but she couldn't even muster enough energy to properly greet the vet's trailered horse. When the doctor pulled into the lane, the trailer rattling behind, Lucy struggled to her feet, belted out her best bray, and then collapsed. If she wasn't in so much pain, we would have laughed at her grand maiden-in-distress act, but by now she was rolling and flogging her head against the hard ground. Her heart was racing, and the vet's first injection of painkiller had no effect. As the second shot began to dull her agony, she lay on her side, her stomach bloated and her mouth open. Several flies landed on her pale gums. She looked dead.

"How do you feel about colic surgery?" the vet asked, suspecting a twisted intestine. Her words struck hard, as I knew the surgery could cost as much as $7,000, with no guarantee it would save her life. I didn't answer the question. I couldn't. That would mean admitting that Lucy was in a fight for her life, and I wasn't yet ready to accept she was that far gone.

Now heavily sedated, Lucy was resting peacefully, her head up and her eyelashes hanging low. It took three of us to roll her onto her feet, encouraging—and begging—her to walk to the barn where we could at least work with some light. She seemed content to stand, though her groggy head drooped to her chest. Listening to her abdomen with a stethoscope, the vet detected only minimal noise. She had been hoping for normal stomach rumbles. We decided to pump her full of mineral oil by passing a plastic tube through her nose and into her stomach. With luck, this would increase her gut activity and loosen an impaction. Holding Lucy's head, I looked into her kind eyes, now dulled by the drugs, and rubbed my hand over her scraped face and nose, stopping to play with her whiskered muzzle. As I leaned my forehead into hers, the tightness in my throat began to thicken. Life without Lucy would be unbearable. She's a habit I can't give up.

Listening to her sides again, the vet looked sombre. The gurgles had only slightly improved. There was nothing more we could do.

"It's up to her now," the vet said. "She has to fight this."

The vet left with instructions to call if Lucy's condition worsened. It was now after eleven o'clock, eight hours since we had rescued her from the field. Carrying two lawn chairs to the barn, Mom and I settled in for what we knew from experience would be a long night.

All horse owners know that colic usually strikes after the vet's office has closed, their pagers tracking them down at movies, restaurants, and Christmas parties. Knowing

Lucy's penchant for dramatics, I had one vet, who was playing basketball, wait three hours before making the hour-long drive. It was thirteen degrees below zero, with twisting, icy roads, and he knew the minute he pulled into the lane she would unload a pile of manure, easing her cramps and pain. Just to prove him wrong, Lucy waited for him to arrive, pull on his winter coat, and don his plastic gloves—then she passed the manure. It was too late. After this trip in the dark, the vet gave her the full works—needles and mineral oil. He wasn't going to risk a call an hour later, and darn it, someone was going to pay for his spoiled evening!

Yes, our Lucy is a great little actress, her colic scenes attracting neighbours who have helped walk her all night, relieving us when our knees have weakened or when she's accidentally kicked us because of the biting pain in her belly. We have slept in sleeping bags on hay bales, taking turns massaging her sides. Thermoses are filled with tea, then refilled with coffee. On one occasion, the stall became an office as I conducted an interview with actor and musician Tom Jackson over my cell phone. I was researching a story about his Huron Carole Christmas concert, an annual fundraiser for the food bank.

"Look, Tom, I'm sorry that I didn't make it to your office, but my mule's come down with colic. I'm talking to you from the barn, where I've spent the night." From the other end of the phone came a chuckle of disbelief.

Some celebrities I have interviewed would have been offended to think of me standing in mucousy manure while I asked them about the personal details of their lives, but not Tom. In fact, he thought it had a special

Yuletide touch, what with donkeys, straw, and a barn. The only thing missing was the babe in swaddling clothes.

Such past scenes played in my mind as Mom and I tucked in for our night watch, both of us concerned over Lucy's lack of improvement. Her lower lip was beginning to curl again, and she was starting to paw the ground—signs that she was still in pain. And then her rump began to quiver, the tremors moving up her sides and along her neck until her entire body shivered like a November aspen. Never had I seen her this bad. We draped two woollen afghans across her back, switched on the heat lamps and shut the barn doors. An hour later, she was still shivering, so I called the vet.

"Just keep her warm. She may just be cold, or it could be a sign she is getting worse. If that's the case, call me back. But remember, sometimes they get worse just before they get better."

I hung onto her words like someone hanging onto a branch dangling over a precipice. At least Lucy wasn't trying to lie down and roll, and her lip had stopped curling. We began to chat to Lucy in sing-song voices, hoping she would relax her muscles, just like she did when I sang to her as a foal. Rubbing her neck, with the brooding lamps casting a warm glow across her back, we waited another hour until her tremors stopped. I knew Lucy was feeling better when she turned her head and watched my hand reach into my pocket, where I often keep a stash of green peppermints. I offered her a hank of hay. She took it and looked around for more. This was a great sign. Minutes later, a gale of flatulence filled the stall. Such a sweet sound, after such a sour night. Her ears now perked, Lucy began to show interest in the donkeys waiting outside on the other side of the paddock fence.

It was 2 AM. For twelve hours, we hadn't left her side. Mom and I limped back to the house, weary and several hundred dollars poorer. I checked on her one last time before calling it a night. This was one sunrise I really didn't want to see. The next morning, Lucy was back to her comical self, nosing my pockets and tugging at my sweater. We'd do almost anything for Lucy, our resident drama queen, but we do wish she'd drop the horror roles and stick to comedy.

Chapter Twenty-Nine

Big Oil

I would much prefer to stare out my window at a windmill. There is poetry in its dance.

Many people who pack up and move to the country are seeking nirvana, hoping to find a place without problems. But it is naive to equate such a move with the great escape. While the sunrises and sunsets come close to perfection, life anywhere is never perfect. Attend any rural town hall meeting, and you will hear complaints similar to what you hear in a city—barking dogs, increased traffic, potholed roads, fears about water contamination, and concerns about pollution, be it burning brush, noise, or oilfield emissions. Such is the other side of country living, and in our case it involves living in the shadow of a sour gas well.

We are "downwinders," meaning we live downwind from a sour gas well and pipeline. When the well—only half a mile from our home—was tested, it was flared, a process in which unwanted or uneconomical natural gas is burned, releasing chemical compounds, many of them toxic. The nighttime fireball lit up our barn, its glow devouring every shadow in the valley. It roared like a jet taking off within feet of our front door, its black smoke invisible against the night sky. These were the obvious inconveniences; what worried us more was what we couldn't see—the invisible cancer-causing hydrocarbons such as benzene and toluene, and the potentially fatal gases such as hydrogen sulphide and sulphur dioxide, one of the main ingredients in acid rain. In recent years, efforts have been made to reduce flaring emissions, in response to public concern about its potential impact on people and livestock. But even without flaring, we sometimes feel as if we're living in a fool's paradise, aware that an accidental leak of hydrogen sulphide from the sour gas well or pipeline could kill us, as well as our pets and the nearby wildlife. Even short-term exposure to low levels of hydrogen sulphide can cause nausea, eye problems, and headaches, as well as respiratory and neurological damage.

Believe me, I did not choose to live this close to such a well. When we moved here, the hilltop across the road was aspen bush and pasture. It is still wooded, and cattle still graze there, but plunk in the middle of the grove is a sour gas well, built five years or so after we arrived. Yes, we did fight it, as did many other members of our community who live downhill from the well, where the heavy hydrogen sulphide tends to collect. But it was a classic David and Goliath battle, with landowners taking on an industry that greases the province's economic wheels—some people even refer to the rotten-egg stench of sour gas as the "smell of money." There's little landowners can do to stop wells, since our rights are limited to several inches of topsoil. The province owns the mineral rights, which it leases out to oil and gas companies.

Now, don't get me wrong. I drive a car. I heat my home with natural gas, and I love a hot bath. I'm not against drilling for fossil fuels. What I am against is having sour gas snuggled so close to residents, especially when no one knows the health impact of long-term exposure to low-level concentrations. For forty years, ranchers have complained that flaring has resulted in their own illnesses as well as dead and sick cattle, but only now is there a comprehensive study underway to determine if flaring compromises the health of livestock and wildlife. Ironically, the study does not include the effects on people.

Sometimes Mom and I try to forget about the well, wanting to believe we're in no danger, but that's tough to do while walking our property with two-way radios strapped to our hips just in case we need to be reached because of a leak or blow-out. Of course, we are expected to evacuate without the animals, as if we should be grateful to escape even if it means returning home to find a barn and house full of sick or dead pets. Our animosity towards this project began the day surveyors arrived on our property, uninvited and unannounced. Seeing their orange vests through the trees, I went outside to find out who they were and why they were traipsing about without first coming to our door.

"Oh, we're tying in your place to where the sour gas well is going," said one of the young lads.

"The gas well? What gas well?" I asked.

"The one up there. On the hill."

That's how we discovered—from trespassers—that we would be the closest residents to the well. What followed was a year of letters, phone calls, community meetings, anger, frustration, and numbness. Labelled by some as "wingnuts," we ignored the verbal blows and forged on, taking our fight before the Alberta Energy and Utilities Board (EUB), the body that regulates the province's oil and gas industry. I knew we would lose, since the EUB rarely turns down a drilling application; its normal practice is to grant the permit, then attach a number of conditions that the company must meet to appease the concerned landowners. But I'll try just about anything once, and I wanted to experience first-hand this process, which was so much in the media because of Wiebo Ludwig and his fight with Big Oil near his home in northern Alberta. His incredible battle—with a cast of colourful characters—is well documented in Andrew Nikiforuk's *Saboteurs*, which won a Governor General's award for non-fiction in 2002. The book is dedicated to all "downwinders."

I wish I could say all my fears were unfounded, that the well and pipeline were installed and now operate without a whiff of rotten-egg smell or any threat to safety. But on one fine spring day, when the leaves were just beginning to green up and the pastures looked like a postcard from verdant Scotland, the pipeline, less than a year old, blew a leak and spewed hydrogen sulphide into the air. Roads were blocked as crews scrambled to repair the hole. Hours before we were notified of the leak, we smelled it, as the gas rolled along the valley and creek, just like I told the EUB it would. Again there were reports, phone calls, letters, anger, and mistrust. Throughout my opposition to this well and pipeline project, I was assured by the industry that such an accident would be rare—how I wish they had been right. The blow-out was the result of human error during pipeline construction. Since the accident, the community has again been assured that safety is a prime concern. But some days I don't feel safe because all the technology in the world—and oilpatch technology has improved by leaps—will not prevent mistakes. To err is human, the saying goes, but sometimes those errors cost lives.

The EUB has noted we have the option of selling our home and moving, but I believe Mom and I have a responsibility to take care of that with which we have been blessed—land, beautiful land. Just like Scarlett O'Hara in Margaret Mitchell's novel *Gone With the Wind*, I believe land is worth fighting for. So we will stay, to protect our valley and our home, in the hope it will not be lost to an ill wind.

Chapter Thirty

Donkey Time

There's something about living with donkeys that makes you slow down a notch or two. Now, donkeys are quite capable of a fast gallop, but they prefer to saunter, tugging at thistle heads, grabbing dandelion blossoms, and chewing on anything that grows bark. Native to rocky deserts, they believe in siestas, standing beneath a broad canopy of leaves, a back leg cocked in repose, with their tails switching at flies and their large ears flapping to dissipate the heat. I'm sure just watching them lowers my blood pressure, as I too start moseying along, taking my sweet time to do a day's worth of chores.

Donkey siestas can come at any time, not just at midday when the sun is high and the winds are low. Most often they occur when I need Raven to move, pronto. Ask her to move out quickly and she's likely to put on the brakes. It's got to be her idea, not mine. And it's got to be when she's ready, even if that means adding several more hours to my day. After all, what's the rush? A donkey can live up to forty years, so there's plenty of time!

We call this languid pace "donkey time," and it's part of a donkey's charm. I tried to warn my friend Julie about this trait—that some people call stubbornness—but she laughed it off.

"Don't worry. I've never had an animal that I couldn't load. And I've loaded everything. Horses, bulls, you name it."

The donkey's role as a burdened creature appears in various languages. The word easel, which bears the load of an art canvas, comes from the word "ezel," Dutch for donkey, and "esel" is German for donkey.

"But have you ever loaded a donkey?" I asked.

"No, but believe me, it won't be a problem."

"Hmmm," I grunted—quietly, so she couldn't hear.

I was moving Lucy and Raven back to Lyle's for about a month, while the oil company drilled its sour gas well near our home. We were downhill and downwind of the rig, and I didn't want to take any chances. If we were forced to evacuate because of a sour gas leak, I wanted to know they were safe and outside the plume.

Boy, were we in for a lot of fun. Neither Lucy nor Raven had ever been trailered. Lucy had last been moved when she was about two months old, in the back of a pickup truck with her mare mother at her side. Now six years old, she had never been off the property since. Raven was also ranch-bound, having never strayed beyond the pastures where she was born five years earlier.

I had Julie park the trailer in the pasture for several weeks, just so the girls could get used to loading. Lucy was a star student, probably because the trailer was perfumed with the scent of horses, reminding her of her mother. Walking cautiously up to the open door, she stretched her head forward to get a good sniff, then stepped up and strolled to the back, never blinking at the echoing sounds her hooves made on the floor. From then on, I didn't bother haltering her. I would simply open the pasture gate and she'd march right up the lane, high-stepping it into the trailer. It was like having her very own playpen.

Raven, however, was an entirely different story. For over a week I begged her to take just one tiny step into the trailer, where I placed a mound of hay and a bucket of crunchies and carrots. Name the bribe and I tried it. After sniffing around the back door for about ten minutes, she would tentatively put one leg in, like a cat dabbing its toes in a pool of water. Then came the next front foot. It would be another fifteen minutes before her hind end followed, her neck stretching forward as she desperately tried to reach the hay in the front-end manger. I never forced her, only encouraged her. During those early lessons, I didn't want her to feel trapped. If she decided to back out, I let her. But still, Raven never relaxed, always keeping her hind hooves less than an inch inside the step-up. She was in, but barely.

"Hey, if she gets that far in, I'll get that door shut," Julie said, her confidence on moving day not convincing me in the least. She had no idea how fast a donkey can move backwards, like a rodeo bull blasting out of its chute. Lucy went in first, not even batting an eye when I shut the divider, confining her to the front end of the trailer. She looked up, hay already hanging out of her mouth, and then returned to filling her belly. Then it was Raven's turn. I tried to think positive, not hesitating for a moment as I walked her to the step-up. Up I went into the trailer, and on went her front brakes. "Come on, girl, it's OK. Lucy's here and she likes it," I said, giving a slight tug on her halter. But Raven didn't care.

I motioned to Julie to let us be. I'd just sit inside the trailer, keep Raven's lead loose, and wait for her to decide it was safe to come on board. Slowly, her front hooves came in. And then, gingerly, she picked up each of her back hooves and planted them with the heels barely inside. What Julie didn't know is that Raven wasn't standing square, that her hind hooves were tucked under her haunches, leaving her rear end about an inch outside. Thinking this would be another moving job done in record time, Julie sprang to slam the door shut. The minute it touched Raven's rear end, she fired backwards, almost knocking the door off its heavy metal hinges. "Damn," said Julie. "We just about had her."

"The bad news," I said, "is that we just proved to her why she didn't want to come in here in the first place."

Now, you can call that being negative. Some may say that donkeys are so smart that Raven could read my mind, which is why four hours later we were still trying to get her loaded. But I prefer to think I just know my donkey. It could have rained for the next forty days and forty nights—donkeys hate rain—and Raven would have still stood outside, preferring a good soaking over one second spent inside that dark prison. We tried stringing ropes behind her rear end so she wouldn't back up; then we ran ropes from her halter through the front window of the trailer and down along the outside, trying to haul her in on a pulley. For the final touch, we waved a flag around her hind legs. But none of this worked. She just stood there, not moving a leg, a muscle, a tendon, or an eyelash.

Throwing up my arms, I started to laugh, noticing that Julie was no longer smiling.

"I guess this is what you might call a tough animal to load," I chuckled.

"No, it's not," Julie said. "Horses that are tough to load rear up, strike out, or kick. But she's just standing there. I don't know what you call this."

"Donkey time," I said. "It's called donkey time."

"You see, Julie, you're still thinking horses," I said. "But she's not a horse. She's a donkey. This is how donkeys refuse. They just lock up and stand there."

Julie didn't look impressed. "If I had Dena here to help me, I'd send you into the house. Then we'd get her loaded."

I didn't know who Dena was, but I was glad she wasn't

around. Resorting to brute force never solves a problem, it just creates one. Sure, you may get the animal loaded that day, but good luck next time. What Raven needed was more groundwork, where I could encourage her to move forward, sideways, and backward without the stress of a deadline. Get control of her legs and movement, and much of the problem would be solved. It also didn't help that the trailer was parked on uneven ground, its rear end several inches higher than its front end. Every time Raven dug in her front end, her hooves would slip downhill, putting her in danger of sliding under the trailer. It was a sure recipe for a wreck. My poor Raven. I looked in her defiant eyes and knew further efforts would be useless.

"That's it," I said. "We're done. I know this lets her think she won, and I guess she did. But there are only so many daylight hours left, and I'd like to get her over to Lyle's before nightfall." If I left within the hour, we could walk the six miles to Lyle's by early evening.

"You're going to walk her over there?" Julie asked in disbelief.

"Yep," I said. "We'll be fine. Donkeys like walking. We'll take our time and besides, it's beautiful out. It'll be quite nice, actually."

"But what about the traffic?" Julie asked, almost in tears at the thought of us being sideswiped by some overzealous driver.

"Look," I said. "She's a donkey, not a flighty thoroughbred. She won't care about the noise. Believe me, I know her. We'll stick to the shoulders and she'll be just fine."

First, we drove Lucy over to Lyle's, where she was unloaded into a spacious paddock. As she trotted along the fenceline, I wondered if she remembered this as the place where she was born. I showed her the old bathtub tucked into the corner of the pasture, which I had filled with buckets of water the day before. Her ears perked at the sight of horses grazing in the next field, and then she too dropped her head to feed. It was time to get Raven.

Julie drove me back home, gave me her cell phone number, and demanded I call if we ran into any problems. She was headed to the local bar—I could almost hear the gossip beginning to bubble about a spoiled and stubborn donkey and her even more stubborn owner. Mom and I packed two water bottles and some donkey crunchies into a small daypack. With Raven haltered, we headed down the road, hugging the grassy shoulder so as not to bruise her hooves. As I knew she would, she ignored every passing vehicle, honking horn, and barking dog. The only thing she flicked her ears at were the roadside thistles, with their delicious purple flowers. Donkeys and mules will drag you across an acre-field to reach a thistle and wrap their tongues around the cactuslike thorns to yank off the tops. You can take the donkey out of the desert, but you can't take the desert out of the donkey!

When we passed the oil company security shack about a mile down the road, a guard emerged, waving his arms like an anxious child stepping off a school bus.

"Donkey, donkey!" he cried. "Oh, what a lovely donkey. I'm from Iran and we have donkeys in our villages. Let me go back inside and get some pizza," he said.

I looked over at Mom. "Do you think the pizza's for us or for the donkey?"

The guard returned, handing us a flat box with four slices of pizza. Still not sure for whom this offering was intended, I slipped the box inside my pack. "There's a park down the road," I said. "We'll stop there to eat."

The guard smiled, never taking his eyes off Raven. He gave her a final pat, then returned to the security shack after bidding us luck with our journey. After our snack stop (we ate the pizza, Raven devoured the rose bushes), we heard a truck slow down behind us. Creeping forward, the driver stopped to roll down his window.

"I don't believe it," he said. "I've heard people talk about 'hauling ass,' but now I can say I have actually seen such a thing." Happy with his own joke, he rolled up the window and drove away. To this day, I don't know who he was.

Finally, we arrived at Lyle's gate, greeted by Lucy, who was nickering and pacing the fenceline, glad to see three familiar faces. It had taken us three hours, but everyone was back together again.

Six weeks later, the trip was repeated in reverse. Lucy hitched a ride in the trailer and Raven ambled down the side of the road, Mom and I in tow. In donkey time, there are no ticking clocks. Things take as long as they take. It's really that simple.

Chapter Thirty-One

Purge the Spurge

What one person calls a flower, another calls a weed. Dandelions in sidewalks are weeds, but a field full of the yellow blooms is a glorious floral bouquet.

There's nothing like a stroll through an open field when the wind curls the orange and oatmeal-coloured grasses, the clouds skip across the sky, and the hawks hitch a ride on the afternoon thermals. On days like these, I like to practise what I call field meditation. I sit on a meadow hillside, my knees drawn up close to my chest, and my body slightly rocking as I keep time with the treetops wavering in the wind. If it's spring, I hike into the hills, where canary-yellow glacier lilies poke through aging snowdrifts, and purple crocuses unfold under a warming sun. The crocuses always remind me of gnomes, their petals opening like a little person stretching and yawning after a long winter's sleep. Come summer, the fields mature into impressionistic canvases of wildflowers blooming in dappled yellows, whites, violets, oranges, and purples. My favourite is the red paintbrush, whose crimson bracts burst like a scarlet sunset over a sea of green.

Several summers ago, a new flower bloomed in our far west fields. Tall and lean, it had blue-green leaves and wore a crown of yellow. It towered over all the other grasses and flowers, dancing in tow-headed circles. I flipped through the pages of my flower guides, searching for its identity, but nothing came close to describing the lanky stem which encased a milk-white sap. I welcomed this new arrival as I would a new neighbour, but then one day a stranger showed up at our door, asking who owned the far field. A field man from the agriculture department, he had noticed our carpet of yellow while driving by on a hunt for noxious weeds.

"Those fields would be mine," I said.

"Well, you've got leafy spurge."

"I've got what?" I asked.

"Leafy spurge. It has a yellow flower."

"Oh, those flowers. I wondered what they were. I thought they were quite pretty."

The weed officer tried not to roll his eyes, but he gave a heavy sigh as his shoulders dropped and he turned his head away. I'm sure I heard a mumble about blasted hobby farmers, or something of the like. Visiting the field with me, he confirmed that we were indeed talking about the same plant. He sentenced the weed to death, warning me that if it wasn't killed, it would crowd out every living thing in its path and rule the pasture like some malicious monarch. If I didn't kill it, the municipality would do the deed with a spray gun, then drop the bill on my doorstep, he said.

"Spray it?" I asked. "When it's growing on a hill and so close to the creek?"

At first the ag man shuffled his feet, then assured me spraying would be safe. Within a week, a masked weed man was tending to our unwanted garden, hosing the plants with some foul-smelling liquid. Gasping for air, the flowers faded, wilted, and then—came back! Full strength and full bloom, with the petals as bright as sunshine, as if snickering at our foolish effort!

I refused to spray again, already feeling guilty about ignoring my conscience. How could I taint the creek that faithfully gurgled at the bottom of the hill? Whether weakened by drought or strangled by ice, it never ceases to run, weaving its way through bog and beaver dams. It's not that our creek is pristine—far from it. In spring flood, it runs wild with rubber tires, pop cans, and plastic gas tanks. Cattle and horses wander its banks, dropping gifts of manure, and I'm sure I've seen Maggie dog squat in one of its many dark pools. But heron fish on this creek, little minnows dart beneath its long reeds, and muskrats rudder their way around logjams and bulrush thickets. No, there must be another way.

I couldn't use the donkey and mule as grazing power, since the spurge's sap would burn their mouths. Someone told me goats—they must have asbestos lips—could take care of it, but that would mean building a goat-proof fence. I could barely maintain three strands of wire, never mind wrestling with page wire and more than a mile's worth of work.

Well, what about me? Thinking I could nip it the old-fashioned way, I spent several days as a bipedal grazer, snapping every flower from its stem, my work gloves sticky with the sap. But it was back-breaking work, and I didn't look forward to adding yet another chore to an ever-growing scroll of summer tasks. So the following summer, I pushed our hulking Husqvarna lawnmower up the hill, squeezing it between spindly tree trunks bordering a woodland trail, and then maneuvered it down another hill before crossing the grassy slopes to the new hatch of spurge. Firing up the orange beast, I began to cut, sculpting a tidy crop square. With no trace of tracks in the long grass, it looked as if the mowed patch had landed there. I laughed, thinking of all the passersby scratching their heads. This could be one for the tabloids, a variation on alien crop circles. I had often watched mysterious green, yellow, and red lights, with no definite shape or sound, pulse overhead at night. So it wouldn't be too far-fetched to think of these fields as Roswell North. Sure enough, it didn't take long for several neighbours to inquire about the squares. "What's going on over there? What exactly are you doing?" As tempting as it was to embellish my wing-nut reputation, I fessed up that I was the creator, that I was in a face-off with leafy spurge. Their faces went blank; their eyes glazed over. Most hadn't heard of the weed, and the others were soon bored by my detailing of its biology.

The following summer, I was eager to check the spurge's health, hoping to find the plants frail and stunted. Surely my cutting had weakened their roots. With no leaves and only short stems, how much food could they manufacture for growth? As the range management experts say, "No shoot? Then no root." But I was horrified to find what appeared to be robust spurge, with more leaves than ever, spiralling in every direction. I was now growing spurge bushes. The plants were so thick I could hardly find a stem of grass. Baby spurge was crawling everywhere.

"Never heard of this happening before," said the weed police on the end of the phone. "Don't know what to suggest. Maybe you should call the agriculture research centre."

My call to the Lethbridge Research Centre opened the door to a whole new adventure with this defiant weed. I was told that the lush new foliage was a sign of stress, that indeed my plucking and pruning was causing the spurge to panic. Determined to survive, it was shooting out growth to counter my attempts to kill it. But I also learned its arsenal was endless—a root system that could sprawl almost fifteen additional feet each year, and extend more than twenty-five feet deep. It gets worse. Each plant produces about 140 seeds and casts them about fifteen feet when the seed case explodes. Each seed survives up to eight years. Native to Europe and Asia, leafy spurge has no natural predators in Canada.

Yikes! Now that I knew my enemy, it seemed hopeless. I was sure my pasture was doomed. Not necessarily so, said Ray Wilson from the research centre, who outlined a new plan of attack—insects, thousands of them! Little black flea beetles that would gobble up the spurge, even while I was sleeping.

"Sign me up," I said.

"Done deal. You're on the list. We'll call you next spring," said Ray, eager to plot another test site. There were no guarantees of success, but I was excited by the prospect of using bio-control. For once, I was receiving critters that would feed and water themselves, hibernate in winter, and actually do some work.

Nine months later, Ray arrived at my door with a plastic container and a big smile. Weeks before, he had screened my field to ensure it would be a happy home for the bugs. Apparently it was a five-star lodge, a perfect flea motel with a south-facing slope and good drainage.

I peeked inside the plastic tub, and several of the beetles jumped out. I couldn't believe how tiny they were. Even with five thousand of them—less the few that escaped—they could have held a party in the palm of my hand. Ray warned me it would take several years for them to gnaw their way through my patch of spurge. Several years? I was sure it would take at least a century, making it the longest smorgasbord on record, but I remained committed. The project wouldn't cost me a cent, and it was environmentally friendly. Besides, I needed all the help I could get.

We set the wee gaffers free, wishing them well on their gastronomical journey. Over the next week, Mom and I made daily checks, curious about our new boarders. We soon discovered that our little beetle friends, officially known as *Apthona lacertosa*, are extremely gregarious, lining up along leaves in a chain of black dots. But for most of the year, they are invisible, preferring to spend their lives underground as larvae. In the depths of darkness, they feed on spurge roots, striking the plant where it hurts the most. The beetles have been with us for less than a year, but before they burrowed down, they savaged about ten plants. Not bad for a month's work, and just think, only several thousand more spurge to go!

Oh well, they fit into Burro Alley just fine, munching away on donkey time.

Chapter Thirty-Two

Snow in Summer

When my fields are dappled yellow with blooming buffalo bean, I know it is safe to plant poppies, lettuce, or sweet peas.

It is the second day of August, and it's two degrees below freezing, with snow predicted for the high country hills and mountain slopes. Snow halfway through summer? Snow at a time when much of Alberta is baking in a drought so bad it has old-timers dusting off their memories of the Depression? Just two days ago, we were wilting under a sun that had wrenched every drop of moisture from the soil. The dogs were squirrelly, digging holes under the trees and pressing their bellies against the dark earth to get some relief. Black crows sat on fence posts, their beaks wide open like the mouths of panting dogs. Red squirrels, who normally use tree trunks as speedways, stretched out on limbs with their white bellies against the bark and their tiny claws gripping for balance. Only the mule and donkey joyously basked in the desert air, but then their ancestry dates back to the wild asses of Africa and Asia, animals used to scorching heat and brittle dry brush.

Well, so much for our heat wave. Today dawned with a heavy snowfall warning, sweeping in a rash of migraine headaches and cranky moods. Lord, this place is crazy. I've often said if you don't have a mercurial temperament, Alberta will drive you wacky with its roller-coaster weather. But it all depends where in the province you live. If home is on the sunlit plains to the east, this forecast of winter in summer may as well be coming from Mars. Chances are no one there will spot a flake of the white stuff. But we live in the foothills, that borderland between the prairies and the Rockies, and I'm convinced our valley is the bull's eye of a local snowbelt. Only two months ago, in late May, I was still up to my knees in drifts, wondering if summer would ever blossom, if we would ever awaken from the slow pulse of winter. The pale season lingered, ever the reminder that life is vulnerable, that life ends, that nothing lasts forever. The first spring robins struggled to find worms and grubs in still-frozen ground. They darted across the snow, their red breasts bursting against the stark white like a summer sunrise. Mom put out bowls of raisins and leftover dog food, nursing the shocked robins through the cold spell, but its cruelty killed dozens of bluebirds, swallows, and other insect-eating birds.

So, after only two months of back-warming sunshine, I detest this return of a winter that obviously never really left. What has me quaking in my snow boots are the furry coats the mule and donkey seem to have grown overnight. Raven hasn't even finished shedding, and again her coat is thickening with coarse hair, and Lucy has added a layer of peach fuzz, her slick summer gloss lasting less than a month. I should have known snow was sneaking over the hills by the way she danced, bucked, and paced along the fenceline this morning. That animal is a walking, trotting barometer. When a storm is on the move, she's nervous, anxious for food. It's as if she fears every blade of grass will disappear beneath an avalanche of heavy snow. I'm sure it's the survival instinct. Eat while it's here; stock up for the big one.

The darkening sky reminds me of a freakish whiteout several years ago when I learned never to turn my back on a nervous animal. It was a late-night blizzard, several days before Christmas: the wind was blowing so much snow that my footprints vanished like a ghost. Heaving several flakes of hay into the wind, I dodged Lucy and Raven, who were pivoting and bolting, churning the snow with their nervous energy. I waited until they returned and settled into their feed, then turned my back and walked through a narrow gate towards the barn. Suddenly, I was struck in the back by what felt like a Mack truck. Knocked to the ground, I heard pounding hooves pass by. My ears throbbed. My heart raced. I covered the back of my head with my hands, waiting for the lethal strike. As the drumming hooves continued, I thought a phantom herd had joined my posse of two. Hours seemed to pass, and then all was quiet. Doing a push-up in the snow, I raised my upper body, pausing to see if I could make out any shapes in the snowy darkness. Wham! A stomp on my back, a hoof landing between my shoulder blades, drove my face deep into the snow, knocking the wind from my lungs. I lay still, too scared to move, wondering if the heaviness in my chest would crush my last breath. I knew I had to get back to the house. Groaning, I eased myself up, anticipating the sharp, stabbing pain of a broken rib. But there was only a numb stiffness in the centre of my back. I stumbled to the house and flopped onto the couch in front of the Christmas tree. If this was my time to move on, I wanted Mom to tell everyone I died happily, watching the tree lights twinkle like diamond stars.

I think of this brush with deadly hooves every time a wicked winter storm moves across the mountains, but I don't expect to be haunted by the memory in August, when the night sky is full of summer constellations. This is a time when the garden should be blooming, when sunflowers are reaching for the sky, when pansies are laughing and nasturtiums are ripe for salad-picking. But instead, the flowers are gasping. With a lean six-week growing season, foothills gardening is never easy. We gave up growing impatiens when Jack Frost turned them black overnight. And if it's not high winds breaking the necks of fuchsia blooms, it's hail ripping leaves until they look like grasshopper feed. We've had summers when we fed frost-nipped vegetables to the mule, and autumns when pumpkins froze solid.

Without stalwart geraniums and petunias, our garden would be anemic, as most plants, like Depression-era farmers, give up trying to carve a living from the soil. At least we can bring the geraniums inside for winter and watch the deer tapping the windows, trying to nip the foliage. If the weather doesn't murder your plants, the wildlife will. Gardens look like prison yards, chicken-wired to keep the deer out. If that fails, nylon stockings stuffed with human hair and tethered to outdoor stakes usually keep the critters away.

Sometimes I think it's best to forget the tame flower garden and enjoy the palette of wild colours dotting the pasture: pink shooting stars, yellow buffalo beans, the prairie rose, and the fiery paintbrush. That way, one doesn't pay much attention to the moody weather, like the pelting rain against my window which is now turning to splashes of snow. I can see the wall of white moving in from the west, the gusting wind rocking the spruce tops across the valley. Just in time for the long weekend. I feel a little guilty—not a lover of scorching heat, I innocently remarked the other day that winter couldn't come early enough. I didn't think the sky gods were listening, but with a daytime high of thirty-five degrees—the coldest second day of August in about sixty years—I'm having second thoughts. I wish I could take it back, but it's too late. The valley is hidden behind a wash of white. We don winter sweaters and light a fire, the smoky curl rising from the chimney to tease the aspens' shivering green leaves.

Please, I beg the creator of all things bright and beautiful, bring back the heat. I promise I won't complain too much. Well, at least not until next week. When the drought returns.

Chapter Thirty-Three

Jesus Donkeys

Peso pushes his broad forehead, its bristly hair the colour of grey barnboard, into my chest. Rubbing the inside of his ear with one hand, I stroke his velvet black muzzle with the other. He rolls his eyes until he's cross-eyed, trying to focus on my hand. I poke a finger inside his mouth, massaging his gums in the space between the incisors and the molars. He sucks on my finger, then lets me curl back his lips. I notice he's missing his two milk nippers; the permanent incisors are just beginning to drop down. "Poor little one," I say, caressing his mop of a forelock. "Makes it tough to chomp winter hay, doesn't it?" Three-year-old mules and donkeys have a tough go of it. They're losing baby teeth and cutting new ones, and their gums are red and inflamed.

Stocky and sassy, Peso is our little one, a miniature donkey given to us by our neighbour John, who wanted no money, just a good home for yet another donkey jack born on his property. He may be called Peso, but he's not as worthless as the Mexican currency. Far from it, he's a dear heart, knock knees, underbite, and all. What he lacks in show conformation, he more than makes up for in character. We could have named him Merrylegs, since his stubby limbs never stop moving, pumping like pistons as he charges across the fields, his wispy tail spinning like a windmill. His bray is nothing like Raven's; her vocal

Like most animals, donkeys prefer to have company, whether a horse, cow, sheep, or goat. There is nothing more forlorn than a lone donkey in a field.

cords resonate with the depth of the Grand Canyon, while his are a shallow shriek, like someone pinging rocks off a tin can. But he's feisty, hoofing a heave-ho at the mule or Raven if either tries to sneak a slurp from his tub of bran mash. He may be little, but he's a giant when it comes to attitude. Napoleon B. would have been a good second name.

But there's something else about Peso that makes him the chosen one, that makes us forgive him when he dances the limbo beneath the bottom strand of fence wire or nips instead of using his lips to pluck a peppermint candy from our hands. He bears the cross on his back, telling the world he is special. It was a donkey that carried Mary to the stable manger on the eve of Christ's birth. And it was a donkey that carried Mary and the newborn babe when they and Joseph had to flee Bethlehem.

What of the brays that shake our valley when dawn comes? Well, the story goes that the donkey's keen ears heard Herod's soldiers nearby, but that he could not awaken Joseph, Mary, or the Christ child. Up until now, the donkey had had no voice, but all of a sudden he was blessed with a miracle—a shattering bray that woke the family and allowed them to escape. From that day on, all donkeys could speak.

It was a donkey that Jesus rode into Jerusalem on Palm Sunday. On the day that He was crucified, it is said, the donkey wanted to help carry the cross, but the animal was pushed aside by the crowds. He waited to say goodbye and, when he turned to leave, quietly shed a sorrowful tear while the shadow of the cross fell across his back and shoulders. So all donkeys, no matter their colour, bear a stripe of dark hair down their back and across their shoulders, and the light markings around their eyes are shaped like teardrops. The marks are to remind us that this is the humble creature that carried the Son of God both to his birth and to his death. Such devotion to the holy child is why some people refer to the shaggy creatures as Jesus Donkeys. In olden days, a mother whose child had whooping cough would pluck hairs from the donkey's cross and hang them in a sack around the child's neck.

Someone, however, forgot to tell Lucy that this newest addition wore a halo. When Peso first came to live with us, he was shunned by Her Majesty. She chased the little grey waif as if he were a coyote runt, nipping his withers. Poor Peso was terrified, tucking his tail between his legs and braying like a fire alarm. We separated the two, pairing Peso with Raven, who quickly fired a hoof at Peso when he thought he'd found a nanny. Raven wasn't keen about her babysitting duties, but she tolerated the weanling, and at least we could rest at night knowing she wouldn't intentionally hurt him. Lucy, like most mules, is easily bored, so she soon grew weary of watching this runty beast from the other side of the fence. When she wandered off to graze elsewhere, I knew she was ready to accept another member into the herd. Within days, the two of them were prancing about, nibbling at each other's muzzles and playing chase games.

Many have given their hearts to donkeys, captivated by their soulful eyes and spunky character. Queen Victoria owned three of them, choosing a donkey carriage as her favourite way to travel. But perhaps no one has given so much as Elisabeth Svendsden, who has devoted her life to improving the welfare of donkeys around the world. In 1969, she opened the Donkey Sanctuary in Devon, England, rescuing ill-treated donkeys and any donkey no longer wanted by its owner. She also travels to the world's poorest communities, where donkeys are used as beasts of burden, often under horrendous conditions. Many suffer short lives because they are infected with parasites, while others are covered with open sores from carrying heavy loads over long distances. Most are undernourished.

I dream of one day opening a donkey sanctuary in western Canada, a counterpart to the one near Guelph, Ontario, which takes in abused, neglected, and unwanted longears. With donkeys living as long as forty years, and some even longer, many are abandoned, left alone in fields, where their hooves grow so long they turn up like shoes on a leprechaun. The animals go lame, but most can be saved with proper care and trimming. They are precious animals: we should, as one vet said to me, "treat them like you would your favourite aunt."

I often think of her comment when Peso and Raven are following me around like second shadows, stealing my gloves if I put them down, tossing my hammer if I leave it on the fence post, and tipping over the wheelbarrow when I turn my back. Special, indeed. I couldn't imagine life without them; a field full of donkeys is a field in blossom with friendship. Never have I owned animals that are so happy to be alive. I truly believe Peso, with his vivid cross, knows he is special. He asks for so little, yet gives so much. He sparkles like a precious gem—a true diamond in the rough.

Chapter Thirty-Four

Canine Costumes

Today the dogs dug up a chunk of deer meat. Buried at the base of a spruce tree, beneath cones and duff, our discovery was likely a cougar cache. We continued our walk at a brisk pace!

Maggie and Georgie are the beloved twins of Burro Alley, their freckled faces and wagging tails greeting all visitors. Like true sisters, they share everything—turkey giblets, dumb ol' sticks, decaying deer bones, frozen chunks of manure, vicious barking duties, and the faded-blue front seat of the truck. But when it comes to a kind word or a soft pat, they jealously vie for our attention. Maggie, the larger of the two, shoves Georgie aside with her fat rump or her bear of a head. Nimble Georgie takes only so much abuse before charging into Maggie, nipping her ruff or standing on her hind legs to deliver a knockout punch with a front-leg jab. Humbled, Maggie pouts in a corner, her head resting on her outstretched paws. It's now Georgie's turn, as she moves in for our ear scratches. Come dinnertime, all will be forgiven, as they swap food bowls, then share the rug at our slippered feet.

Such jockeying makes for a confusing household. Most days I'm not sure which dog is in charge. It's one thing to switch food bowls, but quite another to swap personalities, especially when the trade is batted back and forth like a ping-pong ball. In the flick of a fly, Georgie, the shy tyke, can blossom into a braveheart, tearing through the willow brush after anything that moves and attacking the inside of my car if a passing cat or dog even thinks of looking her way. No dog can slip into the shadows as fast as our George. Turn your back, and she's hot on a rabbit trail, yiking her primitive war cry. Call her name, whistle, or curse—it doesn't matter. When she returns, her tongue is dragging in the dirt and her sides are heaving like fire bellows. We can tell she knows she's ignored our commands by the way she slinks along the ground. Then, as quickly as she disappeared, she wags her tail, smothers our hands in kisses, and reverts to the same brown-eyed coquette that captured our hearts when she was a pup peeking over the lip of the cardboard box.

Then there's Maggie. Remember our bold and beautiful? Well, she's as handsome as ever, even if her rump is as broad as the barn, but she's one of those dogs that's courageous on the outside and cringing on the inside. On occasion, when Maggie is sitting in the truck hoping we'll go somewhere, Lucy moseys over, licking the windshield and nibbling at the side mirrors. Poor Maggie attacks the windshield like a rabid animal, then dives to the floor, shaking as she tries to crawl under the front seat. Not that she would ever back down from an intruder: pity the stranger that threatens to harm her house, her sister, or her people. She can tree a bear like a hound trees a cougar, but given the chance, she would stuff herself in my back pocket, all sixty pounds of her. She is threatening yet timid, a sheep in wolf's clothing. In obedience classes, where she excelled at all the games, she flunked the social graces. One nose-to-nose meeting was fine, but if she was approached by two or more dogs, she'd squat and pee, then try to climb into my lap, only to growl at a lumbering black lab that wouldn't stop barking in her face. But then, they do say dogs take on their owner's personality. Give me space, and I too am easygoing; but crowd me, and I swear my canines grow another inch.

To boost Maggie's confidence, I enrolled her in agility classes, where she raced through nylon tunnel tubes, leaped over wooden jumps, and climbed steep ramps. This was more like it. She was working with only one goal, to please me. The heck with the other dogs, she had a job to do, and she was going to be the best. Ah, a true herding dog, I thought. That's what she needs, to round up sheep as her ancestors did. A stock dog trial was to be staged on a farm not far from our home—the perfect place to introduce her to a flock of woollies. We prepared for the grand event by watching the video *Babe*, the story of a pig that learns how to herd sheep. Both Maggie and Georgie adore that movie, barking with the cast of dogs, geese, and singing mice.

On the big day, Maggie and I grabbed front-row seats on the grass, excited at the chance to mingle with other working dogs and their masters. But it wasn't long before we heard the guffaws and gossip about Maggie's lineage. It seemed our kind was not welcome; you see, Maggie is only half border collie, the offspring of a mixed breeding. Shame on her dad for being an Australian shepherd, passing along his mottled coat and heavy build. This may have been a stock dog trial, but the only breed considered worthy was the border collie, their sleek bodies lying flat to the ground, their alert faces waiting for the shepherd's whistle. Maggie looked like a hog among princes and princesses, a pauper among royalty.

"Don't worry, Maggie," I whispered. "We're just here to watch. They can't kick us out for that." Maggie sat straight, her hefty rump snuggled into my thigh. She looked up at me, her panting tongue working overtime in the noonday heat. "That a girl," I said, giving her a soft pat on her head. "Soon you'll see sheep. You've never seen live woollies before, have you?"

The crowd grew quiet as the herding action moved closer to the bleachers. The dog and flock were in a small dip, working their way up the rise and into sight. "The sheep are coming, the sheep are coming," I whispered. A sheep popped its head over the hill, then a second, and a third, the border collie working wide to the right.

Maggie was looking keen, her body beginning to tremble like aspen leaves in a fall breeze. And then her mouth clamped shut.

Look at that, I thought. Her herding instincts are awakening. Who says a mutt can't herd sheep? And then I heard the growl from deep in her chest. "No growling, Maggie. You'll scare the sheep."

But her ears were pinned flat to her head, and her yellow eyes were huge and round. She crawled behind my legs, dragging her belly along the ground. "This can't be happening," I thought. "She's a herding dog. She has collie in her blood. She's probably related to Lassie."

But there was no denying her fear. Maggie was terrified of the sheep. I removed her from the edge of the field, ignoring the I-told-you-so stares from the crowd. Within minutes, her tail was a happy waving flag, while her nose wiggled along the ground in a search-and-rescue mission for hot-dog crumbs. She jumped into the truck, ready to hang her head out the window where the wind would buffet her ears. Just before I shut the door, we were approached by a young man with a smart and classy border collie heeling at his side.

"Oh, great," I muttered to myself. "What wisecrack is he going to make?"

"I saw what happened back there and I wouldn't feel badly," he offered. "It sometimes takes a dog a while to work with sheep, especially if it's her first time out. I've trained dogs that took weeks to notice the sheep were even there."

I was grateful for his kind words and thankful he didn't blast me for owning an Aussie mongrel. But I also knew Maggie would never be a champion sheep dog. She was spoiled rotten, and I was to blame. She'd had too many nights sleeping at my side, too many roadside snacks, too many hugs, too many hours spent as a couch potato. She knew her place, all right—in my heart and by the hearth.

During our drive home, Maggie rested her head on my lap, arching her eyebrows as she looked up at me, her eyes soft and sorry. I patted her forehead, reassuring her that she was still my best friend. When we arrived home, George raced out the door to greet us as if we'd been gone a year. Maggie lay down, yipped, and began herding her to nowhere in particular. I guess she believes in picking on something her own size.

While George goes along with the game, she can herd circles around Maggie. She deserves a badge of courage for driving home Peso, the miniature donkey, sticking with him as he charges through the trees, leaping over deadfalls and occasionally tossing in a kick with his back leg. She never barks or nips at his heels, and she knows to keep a safe distance from those hard-hoofed legs. I'm sure she could teach those border collies a thing or two. But how would I get her to the stock dog trials? George doesn't particularly like cars. She'll tolerate a drive if there's a long hike at the end, but she spins like a washing machine if she's trapped inside with the windshield wipers clapping. And if a hawk or raven flies over, she sits back, points her nose to the sky, and tracks its wingbeats until it disappears over the horizon. So maybe bird dog trials would be more her thing.

Who knows what travels through a dog's mind, what makes them cringe one day and crow the next. What I do know is that I feel as if I am living with a canine interpretation of yin and yang, and that I am never too sure who is being who. I guess it depends which side of the blanket they fall asleep on, and which side they wake up on.

Chapter Thirty-Five

Muletide Greetings

The deer are yarding up, a sign of incoming heavy snow. Tonight they will lick the bird feeders clean and gobble up the extra alfalfa cubes we leave on the ground. A gift for Santa's deer!

It is Christmas Eve, one of my favourite nights of the year. The sky is stippled with silver stars, a borderless canvas of festive lights. Fresh snow drapes the trees and softens the crunching of hooves as the mule and donkeys move in single file up the hill. I still can't see them, but I can hear their breathing—slow, steady, and deep. There is no need to call them. They have already heard the barn door creaking and me humming Christmas carols. I wait for them, so I can wish them an early merry Christmas, pat their necks, and listen to them munch their hay, a most satisfying sound of contentment.

I shake loose the flakes of hay, the alfalfa leaves settling in the snow like dark exclamation marks. It is the last feed of the day, and I toss in a few carrot-flavoured crunchies, it being Christmas Eve and all. A white puff of steam floats above the heated water tank, and the light from the barn streaks across the snow like moonglow. Further down the valley, my neighbour's barn twinkles, its trim decorated with a rainbow of yule lights. There isn't a dog barking or an owl calling. It is indeed a silent night.

Mules and donkeys are biblical animals, and I am sure they too sense this special time of year. Together we wander down to the shed, where we stand in a row, our butts to the backboards and our faces studying the eastern sky. I am one of many who believe that, on this holy eve, animals talk in human speech after midnight. I have never heard their conversation. I've never witnessed rabbits dancing under a full moon, either, but I've seen their tracks the morning after!

When Christmas morning dawns, I greet the mules and donkeys with a hearty ho! ho! ho! and three tubs of warm bran mash—a gruel of grain, molasses, and salt. They paw the ground, nicker, snort, and crowd one another, jockeying to be first in line. There is much slurping and mouth-smacking as the tummy-warming mash hits the spot. It is minus twenty-five, but it feels warmer with the sun bouncing off the snow. The animals drop their heads and cock their hind legs, facing the fireball now rising against a sky of sparkling ice crystals. A few cavernous yawns, and they settle in for a morning siesta.

Mom waits on the birds, smothering stump tops with sunflower seeds and filling tube feeders with Niger thistle seed. It's a real smorgasbord, with a little Noel mincemeat and slabs of suet tacked to a tree trunk. Within minutes the flocks arrive: boreal, mountain, and black-capped chickadees; blue jays and grey jays; white- and red-breasted nuthatches; downy and hairy woodpeckers; pine, evening, and rose-breasted grosbeaks; siskins, juncos, and redpolls. They cram the perches and platforms and sometimes stand on top of one another, so desperate are they for food. The feeders are topped up at least three times a day, a reliable source of fuel to help our feathered friends survive nights when the mercury sinks to thirty-one below. If it's a clear night, we can hit minus forty, where Celsius and Fahrenheit meet.

A small mound of hay with a sprinkling of crushed

alfalfa cubes is reserved for the mule deer, who are struggling with deep snowdrifts. Like horses, they vie for food, the more dominant ones bunting and striking the others out of the way. Their radar ears never stop flinching; their wet, black noses are always searching the air. Step outside and they vanish with giant leaps, only to return several minutes later after circling the house. Yesterday a lone young doe moved up the hill until she was face-to-face with Lucy, who actually ran over to greet her. They stretched their necks until they were nose-to-nose, their long ears almost touching. A molly mule meets a mule doe. I'd love to know what information they were exchanging.

With the dogs and cats fed, and the barn cat nibbling his way through a double serving of Christmas breakfast, we—the humans—are now ready to sit down to our own festive spread of fruit and yogurt, toasted stollen, and bottomless mugs of cinnamon coffee. I don't know of any farm where the animals are not fed first, even on Christmas. It gives you a chance to check on their health after a shivery night, but it also brings peace, since the donkeys start braying as soon as they see the kitchen light go on in the window.

Unless there's a blizzard battering the slopes, Lucy and I go for a ride in the mid-afternoon, when the sun is the warmest. I dip the metal bit in warm water before slipping it into her mouth, but I leave the saddle behind, preferring to snuggle against the heat from her fuzzy body. If my hands get cold, I shove them between her back and my thighs, sitting on them while she bobs her head on a loose rein. If it's not icy, we trot through the soft powder, the sprays of snow splashing up Lucy's legs and trailing in a wake. What a grand way to celebrate this blessed day!

Christmas week is a time to read and to receive visitors

willing to brave unploughed rural side roads. Even if the city is green, it's a rare Christmas that the foothills are not cozy beneath a quilt of white. The dogs charge through the snow, burying their faces deep as they snuffle for scurrying moles. Inside, we keep a fire crackling and plates full of tarts, shortbreads, loaves, and cherry-topped cookies. Enjoying the holiday bliss, the cats perch on the windowsills, their heads cocked as the birds dart from feeder to feeder.

New Year's Eve brings a glacial sky, with a half moon drifting like a berg of sea ice and clusters of stars bobbing in the dark. The donkeys' whiskers are frosted, their breath suspended in the air like clouds of dandelion fluff. We stand on the crest of the hill, humbled by the vast sky and the magnificent waltzing of the stars. My thoughts float back to those many Christmases at our cabin at Lucy Lake, when at night we would light the storm lanterns and skate on the lake, listening to the wolves howl and the trees pop. I wonder what my dad is doing. Is he skating on some heavenly pond, up among the same stars I am watching? Is he reading another arctic adventure by the light of the same moon I see? Does he remember stoking the fires throughout the night so that we could warm our clothes in the morning, so that we could slip into warm woollen socks and sweatpants? Can he see us now, still enjoying the wilds of a Christmas Eve, in a different home, but still next to a warm fire?

A lone star shoots across the sky in a streaking arc. I whisper to the mule and donkeys that we should make a wish to welcome in the new year. After all, this is a new beginning, a time to remember what has been and to wish for good things to come. After this past year of drought, followed by a rain-soaked harvest, my list unravels like an endless scroll.

First of all, let's start with snow. We need plenty of it. And then a good spring rain, whatever it takes to end the drought cycle. But don't forget to turn the taps off. We don't want flooding. And we need enough warmth to get things growing by May.

May the sloughs be full, and the dugouts and water wells deep. May every colt and calf be born healthy on lush spring grass, and every field of grain or hay be kissed ripe by golden rays. May your horse never throw a shoe or a bucking tantrum. May your saddle tree never break and your cinch stay tight. May your stock never taste larkspur or water hemlock. May your cow not choose a badger hole or steep riverbank as a calving site. May good ranch horses and faithful working dogs never be replaced by all-terrain vehicles. May your combine never suffer a broken axle or loose bolt. May you find the missing tools beneath the seat of your pickup truck. May the mice never nest in your glove compartment. May your hay not go moldy. May your calves and crops fetch top prices. May there always be a place for the family farm.

I feel a bunt against my shoulder, then Lucy's warm breath blowing down my neck.

"What's that you say, ol' girl? A few wishes for you? I'll see what I can do."

Bless my mule with a set of withers, so the saddle doesn't sneak up and pinch her neck when she goes down hills.

Lucy, the greedy critter that she is, nudges me again.

"No, you can't have a sandpile to roll in. With our luck, you'd get sand colic. But I will ask that the mosquitoes, gnats, and face flies be few."

Well, if wishes were stars, I've made enough to add another constellation to the night sky. But, because I am sometimes as greedy as my mule, I have just one more wish.

When it seems like nothing is going your way, may you be blessed with three gifts: binder twine to fix everything that's coming undone; duct tape to repair everything that's falling apart; and a sense of humour to keep it all together. So, from my outfit to yours, a very hearty muletide greeting!

Skunked

I dedicate this story to Bucky, a pet skunk my brother and I used to walk on a red leather harness. Bucky came to us "de-skunked," so both people and pets were safe in his company. He would dig for slugs in the bush at the back of our house, and sometimes we strolled down the street, Bucky at the end of one leash and Jan, our Irish setter, pulling at the end of another. Interesting were the nights when the wild raccoon that frequently visited joined us in the living room with the skunk and the dog. Our family was considered unique, if not downright strange, but we were always the first stop for any injured or orphaned wildlife.

Bucky stayed with us for several years, sleeping at nights in a huge wooden barrel that we converted into a cage and bedded with heaps of straw. One night he escaped, venturing into the wilds on his own. Dad was convinced he was living beneath our cabin, a fine dark place for him to burrow. We left him alone, and I chose to believe that the skunk we occasionally saw roaming our yard was Bucky, even if he didn't respond when I called his name. One day I forgot that all skunks, with the exception of Bucky, had scent glands. Hoping it was him, I ran towards the striped animal I saw rooting in the soil.

"Bucky, Bucky, come here, I know it's you. Oh, Bucky, you're still alive."

Yuck! I was hit dead centre, skunk spray dripping down my red woollen sweater. My eyes watered from the putrid smell, as the rank perfume misted my body. Before I was allowed into the house, I had to strip down, from my sweater to my socks. Into the bath I went, and into the garbage the sweater went. It would be another forty years before I found myself that close to a skunk again.

The cats at Burro Alley were getting out of hand. The place had come with a feral calico queen in the barn. An excellent mouser, she was as smart as a crow and as cunning as the red fox that skirts the edge of our meadow. Never did we worry about mice nesting in our hay. We kept a plate full of cat kibble in one of the barn stalls, where we also put a wicker basket lined with straw and an old tattered grey sweater. She seemed grateful, rewarding us with several litters of kittens a year. Several times we tried catching her in a live-trap so we could spay her, but she was too wise for such an old trick. But something had to be done when our tally of barn cats hit the bad-luck number of thirteen! None of the kittens was approachable. All were born between the barn walls, and by the time they showed their cute faces, they were as snarly and wild as their mother. Occasionally a kitten would disappear, most likely killed by a hawk, weasel, or coyote. The light-coloured ones vanished first, their white and orange coats not blending well in the deep-green orchard grass. But I was amazed at how many did survive, and I began to worry about an outbreak of disease. Mamma cat was also starting to look worn out, dragged down by so many mouths to feed.

"We've got to put a stop to this," I said to Mom one morning. "I'm going to try using the trap again."

Waiting until Mamma left for her daily hunt down

along the creek, I then planted the trap deep in the hay bales, where she sometimes snuggled at night. At the far back of the cage, I placed an open tin of sardines. How could she not be seduced by the rich, oily smell of fish? I snickered as I turned out the light and left the barn. I knew she was foxy, but surely I had outwitted her this time.

The next morning I hurried to the barn to see if I had taken any prisoners. The mule and donkeys were still in the field grazing, so the barn was quiet. Real quiet. Darn. I had hoped to hear her rattling about in the cage. Opening the stall door, I still heard nothing. But as I approached the cave in the hay where I had put the trap, I detected movement and the soft sound of fur brushing against mesh. I couldn't believe it. Not only did I have Mamma cat, but she wasn't putting up a fight. She must be in worse shape that I thought, or else those sardines were worth giving up freedom for. I stepped closer, now bending over to peer into the cage. As my eyes adjusted to the dark, I sensed something wasn't quite right. The animal inside the cage was black and white; I knew Mamma cat to be a spotted patchwork of buff-white, orange, and grey.

My hopes sank like a rock to the bottom of a lake. Now I had trouble. Big trouble. My captive was a skunk, a real beauty, mind you, with a thick double stripe running down his back. But still a skunk. The cage didn't have solid walls, so we were stuck trying to remove the cage without being blasted by spray.

Mom was still sleeping when I left the barn, and I dreaded breaking the morning news. She had warned me that the stinky fish might attract the skunk we had recently spotted exploring our woodpiles. Unwisely, I ignored her. Opening her bedroom door, I heard her roll over.

"Been out to the barn yet?" she asked.

"Yep," I answered.

"Well, did you get her?"

"No, not really," I said, finding it difficult to mask the truth. "I got something else."

"Not the skunk?!" she groaned, suddenly wide awake. "Now what are you going to do?"

"I don't know," I muttered. "Maybe if we cover ourselves in plastic bags, we can get him out of there without getting our clothes sprayed."

Half an hour later, we headed to the barn, two silly fools draped in enormous green garbage bags with thumbtack-sized eyeholes. What we hadn't counted on were the mule and donkeys coming in from the fields for their morning hay. Crossing the paddock, a gust of wind crept under the bags, billowing them out so we looked like green ghosts. Lucy bolted, followed by Raven and Peso, who kicked out and ran, braying and bellowing as they tore down the valley. Something told me this was going to be a long morning, if not a long day.

The skunk was now wide awake, and one look at us was enough to put him on high alert. Stamping his front feet, he did a little dance, the warm-up act for a performance I knew all too well. We may have been wearing protective gear, but our hay was in danger of being ruined. Making a quick retreat to the house, we pondered our dilemma over breakfast. Most people consider skunks to be pests, so I knew it would be tough finding a sympathetic ear. I phoned the local conservation office.

"You want to do what?" the woman asked, almost choking on her morning coffee.

"I want to know how to get a skunk out of a cage without getting sprayed," I said.

"Just take it to the creek and drown it," she suggested.

"No, you don't understand. I don't want to kill it. I want to let it go. You see, I used to have a pet skunk. His name was Bucky. So I can't kill him."

There was a long pause and then an abrupt end to our conversation.

"I don't think I can help you," she said.

Crazy woman, I thought. Even if I did want to drown him, it didn't solve the problem of how to carry him out of the barn in a mesh cage without being sprayed. I flipped through the yellow pages until I found a list of exterminators for cockroaches, mice, bats, ants, wasps, silverfish, bedbugs, and pack rats. But not one mentioned skunks. Well, what the heck, I thought, I'll call anyway. All they can do is laugh, be rude, hang up, or all of the above.

"Sure, we can do a skunk," the polite man said.

"Great, but can you get him out alive?" I asked, placing a lot of emphasis on the word *alive.*

"No problem. We've done it before. It's not that hard, really. Just go out there and cover yourself in a sheet so he can't see your eyes. If he can't see you, he won't spray." Gee, my plastic bag idea wasn't so dumb after all!

Unfortunately, I had an appointment in the city, and I didn't fancy leaving my mom to contend with this problem alone. So I dug deep into my pocket and offered to pay the kind man a fee to come out and do the deed. When I arrived home, I could hardly wait to hear the full story, but Mom's report wasn't exactly a high-adventure thriller.

"He just walked in with a sheet, put it over the cage, picked it up, and took it outside." The drama was over before it started. When the cage door opened, the skunk hightailed it down the hill, while Mom and the pest-buster ran up the hill. The trap was put away in the garage, where it still sits today.

As for Mamma cat, she never had another litter in our barn. One morning she was gone, her plate of food untouched. Her youngsters stuck around, until one by one most of them vanished, leaving a lonely queen to take over the hay-bale throne. She had three kittens, and two of them died. The third one, a gorgeous black and white one with dark stockings, was the first kitten born in the barn that I could touch. Hoping to adopt him as another house cat, I held him every day, waiting for him to be old enough to wean. But before that happened, Georgie dog found him wandering outside the paddock, hidden in the long grass next to a log. I heard the screams, then the deathly silence. To George, the kitten was just a spotted gopher. In seconds, she had snapped his tiny neck.

We buried the kitten in the forest, where filtered light warmed the fresh mound of dirt. Apologizing over and over, I blamed myself for teaching him it was safe to trust. I never saw the mother cat again, but within days a smoky tomcat moved in, and two years later he still rules the roost. And out in the fields, beneath a lodge of deadfall and rotting debris, there lives a double-striped skunk. May we all live in peace—but far apart!

They Make Them Tough

On the inside, Renie Blades is as tough as cowhide, but on the outside, she's all lady. When I think of the classic ranch woman, I tip my hat to Renie.

Living off the land is a gambler's game, each day unpredictable, every decision a roll of the dice. Hail can crush a year's harvest in less than ten minutes, a wild grass fire can destroy haystacks and homes, and a late blast of snow can freeze newborn calves. But most ranchers and farmers wouldn't trade their lives for anything. They are wedded to the land, their vows woven on the wind. There is something about land, that sense of place, that seeps into one's blood and soul and becomes the marrow of existence. It is a devotion that makes for a tough life and tough people.

My ranching neighbours, many of them third-generation cowboys, are portraits of a life spent leaning into the wind and sweating under a strong sun. The land is etched on their faces and on the backs of their hands: creases running like dry riverbeds; scars as craggy as an outcrop; cheekbones as prominent as the grand ol' Rockies; and eyes reddened by the wind and sun. Their faces are maps of their lives, lives that breed legends bigger than the open skies. Legends like Harrold and Maurice King, two bachelor brothers who owned land worth millions but chose to live a humble life in a primitive log shack along Sharples Creek deep in southern Alberta's Porcupine Hills. Their story—which began in

1925 when they left home and settled on the other side of the hill from where their parents lived—speaks of a time when there were few roads and even fewer fences, when ambling cattle set the pace and the weather was the only boss worth listening to. The brothers lived together for sixty years, handcrafting their own tools and building their own barn and home with each corner perfectly dovetailed. They never viewed the world from an airplane, took a holiday, or wore a watch. They lived off what they grew in their garden and hunted in the hills, and on one occasion Harrold even crawled into a bear's den, hoping to snare the hibernating animal. They slept in sleeping bags, cooked on a wood stove, read under a single light bulb, bucketed water from a nearby spring, preferred horses to cars, and watched the stars through holes in their roof. For much of ninety years, this is how they lived, running seven hundred head of cattle on thousands of acres of range and backcountry. Neighbours remember Maurice riding across the plains, his wild and white hair blowing from beneath his hat, with his pants held up and his saddle held together with baling twine.

I never met Harrold and Maurice, but I'm sure I heard their discouraging words when, after their deaths in 1995 and 1996, I climbed through a broken window to explore their rustic log cabin hidden in a coulee. Shelves were crammed with hunting and travel magazines, the pages curled from years of winter dampness. Faded calendars dating back more than thirty years were suspended from nails hammered into the log walls. Dish towels and a mackinaw work shirt still hung from a rope strung across the loft. For all their roughness, the brothers were no hillbilly hicks. They knew the cattle business and they knew all about buying low and selling high. From their initial quarter section, purchased in 1926 for less than $6 an acre, they expanded their cattle kingdom into five thousand acres—land worth $6.3 million when it was auctioned off seven decades later.

Harrold and Maurice may have left us, but there are still working cowboys who prefer a good saddle horse and stock dog to the horsepower of an all-terrain vehicle. And there are others who hang onto tradition, moving their cattle overland between summer and winter pastures instead of trucking them down a blacktop highway.

Art and Betty Webster have been trailing their cattle for more than half a century, moving them in summer from the flat fields around Stavely to the high mountain pastures along the south fork of Willow Creek. Their son, Tony, and his wife, Debbie, now help out, as determined as a west wind to keep their family's history alive in this valley shadowed by the peaks of Buffalo, Saddle, and Coffin Mountains. Telephones are no longer connected by a barbed wire fence and the wagon-rutted trails have long since been overgrown, but the rivers still run high, threatening to sweep calves to their death. Art may curse the busy highways that now interrupt the tradition, but he still smiles with pride when he sees the trailing cattle coming home.

A few valleys away, there are women like Renie Blades of the Rocking P Ranch who can swing a rope, catch a calf, and brand a critter within minutes. She's even faster at castrating the young bulls, performing field surgery with her pocket knife within seconds. She's just doing what has to be done and what comes naturally. Her husband Mac's grandmother and mother were no different, riding the range sidesaddle in split skirts. The women were saddle-tough, handing out orders to the hired men. Today, the Bladeses' daughters are keeping up the tradition, with daughter Monica recently retiring from her work as a stuntwoman. She taught Brad Pitt how to ride like a seasoned cowboy in the movie *Legends of the Fall*, but she was the one who rode like the wind and fell off horses, feats too dangerous for the tender-skinned stars. Her own children now slip their boots into stirrups, having already spent a year in the saddle, in front of Mom, by age three.

And how about Iris Glass, the matriarch of four generations of chuckwagon racing. Born in 1924, Iris, also an accomplished horsewoman, has spent fifty years on the circuit, going down the road with her husband, sons, and grandsons, working the outriding horses, checking the equipment, and always cheering on the family's trademark black-and-white checkered wagon. As tough as wagon reins, she's the backbone of the family, staying strong even when the daredevil sport killed her youngest son, Rod, and her son-in-law, Richard Cosgrave.

Then there's my friend Marilyn Halvorson, who runs an outfit of cattle on land homesteaded by her father in 1930. An only child, she grew up hitching Bud and Bill, her father's team of horses. Together they would rake the fields and haul the hay. She learned to drive the tractor when her feet could barely reach the pedals, and in winter months she tended to the home's three wood stoves. Now on her own, with no hired help, Marilyn still splits her own wood, lives sleepless nights in spring when the cows are calving, brings in the hay, mends the fences, pursues escaped bulls, rounds up strays on horseback, and nurtures vegetable and flower gardens. Her land is her sanctuary, and she never plans to leave.

There's Ed Pugh, who, despite his eighty-plus years, rode like a youngster, as lean and nimble as when he began trailing bucking horses to the Calgary Stampede in 1946. Ed and his buddies would drive more than three hundred wide-eyed broncs to the city, fording rivers, stirring up coulee dust, sleeping beneath a chuckwagon, and braving summer thunderstorms. His face was flushed by years under a hot sun and driving wind, and his smile was honest, that of someone who lived the only life he ever knew—or wanted. Ed rode the short-grass hills around his Bar X7 Ranch in Dorothy—his family makes up half the population of this abandoned town southeast of Drumheller—since he and his wife, Edna, traded cattle for their house. That was in 1935. Until his death this spring, he was still working the rodeo chutes, sorting broncs and flagging gates, and running a herd of cattle. May his spurs jingle forever in those back draws and bleached hills.

God willin', Morris Erickson is still riding the range, drifting free as a summer cloud. Morris has worked most of his life as a range rider, moving around like a homeless mustang, breaking a few colts here and working some Herefords over there. Like his friend and neighbour, the late Harrold King, Morris roped bears and coyotes just for the fun of it. He's never longed for his own place, preferring to pack memories rather than mementos. He's bedded down in barns, relying on the horses' warmth to thaw out his frozen fingers, and he's stuffed his boots with newspaper when the temperature hit fifty-eight below. Almost eighty years old, he reckons he's as wild as an eagle, his spirit owned by the horses and the hills. Morris is a man truly wedded to the land.

I may not be cowgirl-tough, but I too cherish land, its strength a much-needed anchor for me during chaotic times, its moods and power keeping me humble. As cowboy philosopher Will Rogers said, "God ain't making any more of it." As long as there is land, horses to gentle, and cattle to move, there will be cowboys and cowgirls. May they continue to be tough so that they can ride out the bad times and tell their stories during the good ones.

Chapter Thirty-Eight

Ruffled Feathers

We looked down at the ruffed grouse lying on our dining room floor. Yes, lying, as in sprawled out dead. All around us were shards of glass, spearing our carpet and stabbing our chairs. Moments before, the grouse, as if on a suicide mission, had rammed our living room window, imploding the double panes into thousands of pieces that scattered like shrapnel. This was not the year's first dead "fool's hen," a nickname for these mountain chickens that display no fear of people. In fact, it was the third. The other two didn't break the windows; they just cracked them, then fell like stones from the sky, landing on our deck with bloodied beaks and broken necks. While we cherish our southern exposure and view of the meadow and spruce hill, we often think we would have been better off in a windowless cabin, or at least one with panes as small as portholes. As bird lovers, it's hard for us not to feel guilty every time we hear that heavy thud against the glass.

We have tried hawk silhouettes, and we have leaned aspen saplings against the windows so their branches sprawl across the pane, breaking up the reflection of clouds and sky. But neither of these tactics has reduced the collisions. One evening, just when the light was turning into a shroud of mist, a great grey owl toting a mouse in its beak smacked into the pane. It dropped the mouse, then retreated to a fence post, where it perched for

I hate to see a dead animal go to waste, so we were going to leave the broken-necked grouse for the coyotes—until a neighbour requested them for his cooking pot.

several minutes smoothing its ruffled feathers. Red-tailed hawks have shattered the windows, and kestrels have used the panes to kill smaller birds, chasing them from the bird feeders into the sky of glass and grabbing them for dinner.

For a small bird, like a chickadee, nuthatch, or pine siskin, there's usually just a tap, a small knock on the head that sends it to a branch where it recovers with a few blinks and a shake of its head. But for the larger birds, like grosbeaks, it's not so easy. The impact usually knocks them to the ground, where their heads become buried in the snow. That's when Mom and I step in as Florence Nightingales. With only a few seconds to save them from shock and suffocation, we quickly place their trembling bodies into a shoebox kept in our mud room. The bottom is layered with paper towels, and once the bird has settled we cover the box and leave the bird alone in a darkened and warm room, usually the bathroom, where the cats are not allowed. Rarely do we lose a bird. Their eyes can be glazed and half-shut, and their hearts beating so hard their bodies vibrate, but in less than an hour they are usually ready to fly. It's a magical feeling to hold such a small creature in the palm of your hand, its warmth like a fuzzy mitten. The grosbeaks tilt their heads, looking up at you with dark, wet eyes. Gripping with their claws, they work their way to the edge of your hand, where they perch before taking flight. My heart flutters with each wingbeat until I see the bird fly straight and land on steady legs. It's always a delight to free a bird, each one a small miracle.

I wish I could say that all the injured birds have recovered, but that wasn't the case with a downy woodpecker, the smallest of all woodpeckers. The poor thing. If only it had died on impact, but instead it tried to stand up, its head leaning far to one side. Its long tongue hung out into the dirt. Holding the crippled bird, we wet its tongue, watching half of it recede into the bill. But minutes later it slid out again. We propped the bird up in the shoebox, but an hour later he had not improved. Perhaps he just needed more time, to allow the swelling in his head to go down. So we packed him up and made the hour's drive to a wildlife animal hospital near Madden, northwest of Calgary, where there are no line-ups or waiting lists.

Built in a donated and renovated church, the Rockyview Wildlife Recovery Centre is a godsend for injured and orphaned animals. It was the dream of biologist Dianne Wittner, who truly believed in the slogan, "Build it, and they will come." Since the centre's opening in 1993, its team of volunteers has received thousands of animals, with admissions increasing from 149 in 1994 to 1,421 in 2001. Their patients, most of them rehabilitated and returned to the wild, include hawks, owls, ducks, songbirds, beavers, fawns, prairie hares, fox kits, coyote pups, baby skunks, and porcupines. The majority are victims of road-hits, cat and dog attacks, poisonings, or collisions with power lines. Those that cannot be saved are humanely killed—as was the case with our downy woodpecker.

After several days of care and feeding, the little guy still couldn't hold his head straight. After a veterinarian diagnosed his condition as permanent, he was put to sleep. It was a story with a sad ending, but the following summer there were five happy endings when the centre successfully raised and released our orphaned nest of barn swallows.

Each year since our arrival at Burro Alley, two barn swallows have nested in the shed, high on a beam within inches of the metal roof. Their babies stretch their scrawny and naked necks, panting in the midday summer heat reflected off the silver roofing. The larger they grow, the braver they become, inching their way to the rim of the nest, where they precariously teeter like a pebble on the edge of a precipice. Quite often I have rescued one or two from the shed's dirt floor, their fragile bodies inches from the donkey's hooves and at risk of being an easy dinner for the barn cats. I keep a small stepladder in one of the empty stalls, just for the purpose of returning the hatchlings to their nest.

One afternoon I found two of five babies alone on the floor, the other three huddled in unusual silence in the nest. Opening the stall door to retrieve the ladder, I discovered both parent swallows dead. One of the barn cats sat nearby, his tail twitching. It wasn't difficult to figure out what had happened. With the babies on the floor, the adults swooped down, trying to drive off the stalking cat. Coming within a hair's length of his claws, the birds were easily swiped from the air. With both adults dead, the babies were doomed to death. Climbing the ladder, I cut down the nest, returning the two fallen birds to their siblings, all of them now dangerously dehydrated. During the hour's drive to the wildlife centre, we frequently stopped to slip an eye-dropper of water into their beaks. When we lifted the shoebox lid, the birds, still stuffed in their nest, squawked for food, their demands deafening in the small space of the car.

At the centre, Dianne had dinner waiting—for the birds, that is. Each one gobbled down a special blend of protein, their ruckus growing louder the more food they received. When we left, the swallows' eyes were bright, wide open, and alert. This time, I had a good feeling. Several weeks later, Dianne sent us a photograph of the birds, letting us know that all had survived and flown to freedom. Thankfully, swallows do not have to be taught how to find food. As soon as they can fly, they are ready to catch insects on their own.

Gradually, we have tried to bird-proof our house. The window shattered by the grouse was replaced with a stronger pane, one that has proven its worth by remaining in one piece after several grouse attacks. We taped cut-outs of owls to the glass, after a neighbour said birds are smart enough to notice the flying hawk silhouettes never move—an obvious and unnatural pose. Because owls perch for hours, the birds are convinced those cut-outs are the real thing. Outside, above the windows, we have dangled almost anything that will flutter or deter collisions: dry reeds, clay mobiles, evergreen boughs, and strands of taffeta. For two people who live like hermits in a deep-woods monastery, our home sure looks like a party house. Long strips of red and silver tinsel flicker in the sunlight and crinkle in the wind, sounding like footsteps crunching across dry grass. Canary-yellow hawk kites swing from the log beams above our kitchen panes, and twirling wind-catchers spin in a circus of colour outside our glass deck doors. Welcome to Mardi Gras year-round!

Some people call our place the birdhouse; I like to think it's because we are bird-friendly. But some days, when I stand back and watch all the paraphernalia waving, clanging, and clattering against our windows, I suspect it has more to do with us—the two cuckoo innkeepers.

Chapter Thirty-Nine

T. S. Eliot would have cherished a cat like Hud, placing him centre-stage in his parade of beloved Jellicle felines. Move over, Mr. Mistoffelees and Rum Tum Tugger! After all, he is a real trouper!

Hud

He may look like a regular overstuffed brown tabby, plump of jowl and thick of thigh, but mediocre he is not. Hud is one of a kind, magic on four paws. I don't know how many lives he has used, but I'm sure it's more than nine. He's been sliced by a car engine, torn by tomcats, chased by donkeys, pelted with stones, attacked by a weasel, and gnawed on by a dog. But what makes Hud truly special is his blindness. For a cat with no sight, he sees so much, enjoying life's bounties and teaching me that one can see through chirping songs, gusty winds, crackling leaves, springy grass, wet puddles, warm sun, cold snow, and, of course, squeaky can openers.

When Hud first came into my life, he was full-sighted. He chose me, pitter-patting through my open door and climbing onto the end of my bed as if he'd slept there since he was a kitten. He was a filthy street cat, a tramp, begging at every doorstep and leaving his calling card on every doorway. His territorial marking didn't stop at the stoop. He sprayed my white walls, my hardwood floors, and anything else he felt like backing into with his raccoon tail quivering like a flag. The insides of his ears were black as coal dust, a sign of ear mites, and he had scratched one until it was raw and bleeding. A monster when it came to eating, he inhaled every morsel, like a squirrel stuffing its cheeks with enough food for a winter cache. I did everything to discourage his presence: I cursed his tom-hood to his face, sprayed him with the garden hose, tossed pebbles at his tail, and ordered him to take his vagabond ways elsewhere. Already owned by three house cats, I declared my inn full, but the same determination that kept this stalwart cat alive kept him yowling outside my window until I gave in, allowing him to sleep on a towel at the foot of my bed.

One day he arrived at my door earlier than usual, his neck and shoulders matted from deep oozing gashes. Seeking warmth, he had snuggled against the warm engine of a neighbour's car. With a turn of the ignition key, his skin and fur were snared, sliced, and gouged by the moving parts. I washed his wounds, listening to his grateful purrs and watching his mighty paws knead the wool blanket I placed beneath his battered body. He was a young cat, but his black toe pads were tough as dry leather from his endless journey to find a home. I named him Hud, after the reckless maverick played by Paul Newman in the movie of the same name.

Of course, now that he had a name, Hud moved in full-time. No longer a back-alley hobo, he was now the prince of pillows. A visit to my veterinarian took care of his ear mites, and also his tom-hood, and thus his obsession to perfume my house with his signature scent. But he never got over his food addiction, eating as if each bowl might be his last, as if at any moment I would toss him back to the streets. He grew and grew, his cobby legs as thick as tree stumps, his face as round as a full moon, and his belly as bloated as a cow on wet grass.

But oh, was he happy! Waddling down the street, he would roll onto his back for every laughing child, chasing after them until they reached down to scratch the top of his head. Everyone loved him, even the neighbourhood dogs, who didn't dare curl a lip in his presence. For several years, he visited the infirm in a long-term care centre, never scratching when patients grabbed his fur and twisted it in a tight knot, and never biting when they made rude comments about his hefty weight. His relaxed body rested like a rock in their laps.

"Oh, Thud, you're so heavy," one lady cried.

"Here, I'll take him from you," I said. "And his name is Hud, not Thud."

"Hud? Well, I certainly think Thud is a better name," she remarked. With Hud now tipping the scales at more than twenty-five pounds—about three times what he should weigh—I could not have agreed more.

Hud remained a popular visitor until I moved to the country, more than an hour's drive from the health care centre. Never a fan of cars—I'm sure the revving engine gave him flashbacks to the night he was carved up—Hud would have staged a revolution against a two-hour sojourn on a highway crowded with growling trucks. Besides, he'd found another hobby, one that quenched his husky appetite. Here, at his front step, were fields of squirming mice, moles, and pocket gophers. Hud was convinced he'd found a heaven on earth. Of course, he had to prance home with his catch, dumping it on the porch so all could see what a wonderful boy he was. After much praise, he would gulp the animal and greedily head back to his killing fields. One morning he retrieved seven mice, at which point I put him inside, his belly swollen with the litter of chewed rodents.

Hud took to farm life as if he'd been born in the barn. He sunned himself on the cattle chute and yowled at the feral queens, recalling his days as a princely stud.

He followed us on walks, ploughing his way through the knee-high meadow grass and climbing our pant legs if it was too tall and wet. In the far fields, he preferred to straddle my shoulder, where he felt safe and had a bird's-eye view of his kingdom.

Hud's joyous life continued, until one day I noticed a mark on his eyeball, a gouged hollow that looked as if it had been scratched by a twig. He was squinting and in recent days had spent more time curled up on my bed than he had roaming the outdoors. The vet diagnosed chronic inflammation in both eyes. For months, Hud was treated with eye drops and pills, but his eyesight gradually dimmed. When one eye ulcerated, I had to wake him for a treatment every three hours. Grateful for any pain relief—even at 3 AM—he would purr as I squeezed the drops into his inflamed eye. Hud eventually lost that eye, when the weakened ligaments holding the lens in place gave out. Before the eye was surgically removed, I stroked his head, committing to memory the beauty of his emerald eyes and how they sparkled like fresh mountain lakes.

Hud's recovery was amazing, a wonderful example of how animals cope and adapt to new situations. He romped about like a youngster, as if he were better off without the sick eye. No more eye drops. No more stinging ulcers. He could still hook a mouse, detecting movement and shifting shadows with his one foggy eye. What a warrior!

Two years later, Hud is now blind, his remaining eye a dull grey. He no longer catches mice, and I can't remember when he last leaped onto the cushioned bar stool or sprang to the countertop. He bumps into anything that wasn't there before and often smacks into the door frame before finding the entrance. He sits and stares at walls, ignoring the avian landing strip around the bird feeders and prods the carpet with his whiskers and nose, in search of his food bowl. Wandering outside has become a risky adventure, ever since he was attacked by a ferocious weasel. Hud has dodged donkey hooves and tricked coyotes, but this time he almost fought his last battle. Ambushed in long grass, he couldn't shake the snarling creature off his back. Weasels can be nasty varmints, clawing and biting their way up an animal's back until they reach the neck, where they strike a fatal bite. With full eyesight, Hud might have had a chance, but he was fighting a creature he couldn't see. Screeching in pain, he caught the attention of the two dogs, who ran to his side, barking and growling as the weasel darted through the meadow's thick sedges. That night, I bathed his wounds with peroxide, counting the lives he's lived and counting our many blessings!

Curtains may have dropped on Hud's eyes, like thin ice clouding a deep trout pond, but in many ways his world remains a pool of senses. His spirit marches on, as he bunts open the screen door with his broad head. It's another day, and there's wet dew to shake off his paws, clicking grasshoppers leaping at his toes, and succulent greens to nibble. This is how he now sees his world, and by sharing his shadow land, Hud has taught me to feel, listen, and taste such small yet large wonders as the dizziness of a single leaf twirling to the ground, the muffled buzz of a bee deep inside a flower, and the sweet freshness of a meadow morning.

Hud and I still take long walks together; I just go a little slower so his paws can feel my footsteps. He's a gallant lad, and he needs to know that after all these years, just like Paul Newman, he can still land on his feet.

Chapter Forty

It is the end of January, but the day is as mild as June. Ambling up the hill is a bleary-eyed black bear.

Bear Wisdom

It was a sultry night, the air heavy, still, almost suffocating, the wicker blinds not even trembling against the open window. I lay naked on the bed with the sheets tossed aside, staring at the ceiling, too lazy even to read. The clock beside my bed read ten past midnight.

At first, the clanking and clunking wasn't all that noisy, but then came the crashes, like falling china and breaking glass. What the heck was that? And why aren't the dogs barking? Then, another crash. I sat up, thinking perhaps it was Hud, blindly strolling along the top kitchen shelf, knocking knick-knacks to the floor as he tried to navigate a path strewn with trinkets.

"Is that you, Hud? Are you OK?" I asked, fumbling for the crutches beside my bed. Still recovering from my broken hip, I was confined to the first floor of the house, unable to take a single step without the crutches. Frustrated and helpless, I had no idea how I was going to retrieve Hud, if indeed he was disoriented and roaming high above the cupboards. I flicked on the kitchen light, but Hud was nowhere in sight, and not one of my barnyard figurines was out of place. Mrs. Cow, Mr. Pig, Master Horse, Watermelon Raven, Sunshine Mule, and the Brighty donkeys—all were there, staring down at us from the lip of the shelf. Hobbling into the living room, I studied the bookcase. Everything was in its place. And there, snoozing in his favourite soft chair, was Hud, his leathery nose tucked under his big front paws.

Well, maybe what I had heard came from the outside deck. Perhaps the flying squirrels or barn cat knocked over a garden pot. I shuffled over to the sliding glass doors. We'd left one door open, hoping the night air would eventually cool and drift through the screen. The kitchen light cast a faint glow on the deck. At first I didn't see the dark face studying me from behind the pot of purple and white petunias. But as my eyes adjusted to the low light, I could make out two beady eyes, a brown snout, and a prune-sized nose. Standing just feet away, on the other side of the thin screen, was a black bear, his head lifting in the dark as he sniffed my presence. Needless to say, I felt somewhat vulnerable standing there stark naked and propped on crutches. To shut the outside glass door, I would first have to slide open the screen, then try to drag the door shut across a warped track, all with the bear less than four feet from my arm. Instead, I backed away, waving my crutches.

"Go on now," I said in my most polite voice. "Go on."

The dogs took this as a cue to bark, convincing the bear to descend the stairs he had climbed to the deck.

Catching a whiff of his scent, the dogs went berserk, jumping in the air and yiking like a pack of hounds.

"What's going on?" Mom asked, appearing from downstairs to investigate the midnight pandemonium.

"Just the bear. He was on the deck, but he's gone now. You might want to shut that deck door, though."

Heading back to my bedroom, I was still baffled by the sound of clanking china. It had sounded so close, a lot closer than the deck. Before switching off the kitchen light, I made one last inspection, my eyes darting back to the side window.

"Just a minute," I said. "Look. The screen's pushed in."

Sure enough, the flimsy screen was no longer attached to the window frame. The bear had shoved it in, knocking aside a set of salt and pepper shakers. Crashing to the counter, they had smashed into an assortment of glass jars. Straightening the toppled glassware, I noticed deep grooves embedded in the sill: sharp furrows left by bear claws. I ran a finger along them, a finger so tiny compared to the bear's curved claws. With the bear this close, I couldn't believe the dogs hadn't barked. Perhaps it was too close, leaving them speechless, just as Mom and I were now, both of us wondering if the bear could actually stuff his entire body through the window. I shuddered at the thought of being trapped inside my bedroom on crutches while down the hall a bear wreaked havoc in the kitchen. This wasn't the first bear to appear at our window, but it was the first one that tried to crawl inside.

Because we live in bear country, we're careful with our food, never feeding the dogs or cats outside, and removing bird feeders after the last snow. But on this night, we had fried a trout, and I guess its oily smell wafted through the open window. Not to mention the bag of ripening bananas sitting on the counter, just a paw's reach from the sill. As hot and stuffy as it was, I shut all the windows. "Just in case he comes back," I said.

The bear did come back, but not until the following afternoon. And *he* was a *she*. Maggie and Georgie chased her, but she retreated only so far before turning around to stare them down. The bear had good reason not to leave—high up a tree was her cub, its arms wrapped around the trunk, its mouth wide open in a pitiful cry. Knowing she'd never leave without her cub, we put the dogs inside. Moments later, the cub slid to the ground, like a climber rappelling down a cliff, then bounded off with mamma.

We have little fear of bears, having spent so much time in Ontario's north, where they are as common as blackflies. But we do respect their power and learned long ago to give a wide berth to a mother with cubs. More than once we've waited inside the parked car because a pair of cubs was sitting smack in the middle of the trail to our cabin.

Like here at Burro Alley, the bears in Ontario would come to our back door, smelling wild raspberry pies cooking on the wood stove. Using their long claws, they would hook open the screen door, only to have it slam in their face because of the heavy spring catch. If that didn't send them running, then Mom would chase them, threatening to whomp their hefty rear ends with a worn-out corn broom. On several occasions, with particularly stubborn bears, we struck up a bushland percussion of banging pots and pans, creating enough of a racket to send them scampering for quiet cover. My brother and I often met bears on the trail, especially when we were sent to get water from the rocky spring. But rarely did we see their faces, just their bobtails as they scrambled off the path. Never did we have a bear turn ugly.

Lucy, however, does not share our relaxed attitude towards bears. One sniff of bear and she paces, snorts, and blows air through her nostrils, sounding like a surfacing whale. One day while we were riding along a cutline, a bear appeared suddenly, standing on its hind legs in waist-high grass. It stood dead centre in front of Lucy, right in her blind spot. Quickly, I turned her in a circle, giving the bear enough time to leave the trail. As we continued our ride, Lucy remained relaxed, her ears flopping back and forth. But as soon as we reached the spot where the bear had been feeding, her ears shot forward and her muscles tightened. Softly, I urged her on with a squeeze of my legs, driving her forward on a loose rein. I could hear the bear snapping branches, but I kept my eyes focused ahead. Lucy forged on, but it was several minutes before her muscles softened.

With so much literature and art depicting ferocious open-mouthed grizzlies, it's not surprising that many of us grow up fearing bears, despite the fact that most of us also grow up with teddy bears, relying on their soft faces to ease our insecurities. Ironically, it is our fear that often makes a bear aggressive. My friends Charlie Russell and Maureen Enns have discovered that it is possible for people and bears to live in harmony, especially if humans can learn to adopt non-aggressive behaviour. Having spent six years studying brown bears on Russia's remote northeast coast, the couple documented their pioneering work in the book *Grizzly Heart: Living Without Fear Among the Brown Bears of Kamchatka*. Charlie, a naturalist who has a deep and spiritual understanding of animals, walks with the bears, holds their massive paws, and reaches inside their mouths. Maureen, a photographer and artist, shares these experiences, mimicking the bears' vocal ranges and dropping to all fours if a bear seems unsure. Once fearful of bears, she learned that many of our fears are built on misconceptions. Together, Maureen and Charlie are trying to make the world a safer place for bears. For Charlie, who grew up near Waterton Lakes National Park in southern Alberta, this work began forty years ago, when he and his father, renowned author and outdoorsman Andy Russell, began filming grizzlies in the wild. For three years, from 1961 to 1963, they shot the documentary *Grizzly Country*, which toured to sold-out audiences across North America. Throughout the filming, they were never armed, and their footage of nursing bears proved that not all bears viewed at close proximity are dangerous. Charlie went on to study the white kermode bears on British Columbia's Princess Royal Island (he writes of this experience in his book *Spirit Bear*) and later established the Khutzeymateen Valley in British Columbia as Canada's first grizzly bear reserve.

Charlie warns us not to emulate his actions, but he does encourage us to try and understand this often misunderstood animal. In our mountain parks, black bears are protected, but once they roam on private lands they are in the crosshairs of anyone who wants to kill them. One Alberta conservation officer told me he considered the bears to be mere "pests, like gophers." It is an attitude I do not understand, and one far removed from respect. In traditional Native cultures, bears were revered and yes, even feared, but they were also respected for their intelligence. I once sat with a Native hunter, who described to me how he had to kill a black bear because the two of them were trying to live on the same hill.

After he shot the bear, he sprinkled tobacco at the site, thanking the bear for giving up his life so that he might stay and have food to eat.

While the survival of bears depends largely on changing human attitudes, it also hinges on habitat protection. I fear for the bears who find their territories infested with development from homes, expanding townsites, and resource industries. The bears desperately need some place to go. Like the cougars, they too are being pushed into inhabited areas, where they often die because of conflicts with people. Mom and I try to do our part by declaring areas of Burro Alley off-limits to both us and the dogs. These are places where the buffalo berries grow thick, where the sedges and cow parsnip are lush, and where dead logs harbour ants and wasps. From our window, we can sit and watch the bears rest on their haunches, the parsnips folded in their laps. And from our back deck, we can hear stumps being toppled as the bears rummage for insects. We cannot always see them, but we take solace in knowing they are there.

Chapter Forty-One

Wilderness Hands

The land shapes our hands and our lives.

Never have I seen eyes grow so big on someone so small. My cousin's daughter Jessica screamed and danced as if she'd caught a glimpse of Santa Claus sledding across the sky behind his reindeer. But what she had spotted was a deer, a solitary doe emerging at the edge of the forest.

"A deer. I just saw a deer. Oh, isn't it wonderful! I just saw a deer."

"Yes, Jessica, it is wonderful," I said. "You're a very lucky girl."

"I'm going in to get my camera," she yelled, not knowing her ruckus sent the deer crashing deep into the woods, its heart pounding every time she screeched. But a lesson in the etiquette of wildlife watching could come later—what was so delightful was to see this seven-year-old's genuine thrill at sighting a mule deer pruning willow bushes so close to our home.

Jessica and her sister Anne were on holidays, two kids from the suburbs awestruck by the wild animals roaming our backyard. They didn't care about their mosquito bites, or about the thistle and rose bush scratches on their legs. They were having a ball, scrambling through the fields, where they found blue jay feathers, mottled butterflies, and all sorts of creepy crawlies. Jessica and Anne had come to Burro Alley hoping for a country vacation, and by golly, they were having one! They shovelled manure, rode Raven bareback, fed Peso peppermints, and chastised Lucy for laying back her ears. Down along the Sheep River, they spent an afternoon puddling about and damming a rock pool. Then they watched a herd of bighorn sheep graze high on a hillside. Two days before they left, a young bull moose wandered within feet of their bedroom window. Each evening, they wrote and sketched pictures in their daily journals, recording the magic of their holiday.

When Jessica and Anne left, they waved goodbye to the animals, promising to come back soon. I hope they do. Children need to know that nature can be a precious friend. Whether they walk along a wild river or stroll through a city park, it doesn't matter, just as long as they realize they are part of nature, not separate from it. It helps if parents teach these lessons, but sometimes lasting influences come from adults outside the home—be it friends, relatives, or teachers. My parents immersed my brother and me in the natural world, but others also left impressions as precious as fresh tracks in the snow.

Today, Canadian wildlife artist Robert Bateman is an international celebrity, but I remember him as someone who helped shape my love of the land. Bob likes to say he knew me before I was born. I guess he's right, since he was friends with my parents long before I popped into this world. Searching for great horned owls, Bob frequently visited my parents' property, craning his neck to spot the owls hugging the trunks of pine trees. Algonquin Park was a mutual passion for Bob and my parents, with its mosaic of wild lakes hidden like deep secrets behind rocky outcrops. For three summers, Bob worked at Algonquin's wildlife research station, while my father taught canoeing at the park's Camp Tamakwa and Camp Ahmek.

I don't exactly remember the first time I met Bob, but

my recollection is of a boyish naturalist who lived near the Niagara Escarpment in a hillside home among the rolling woods and farmland. In his dining room was a Japanese garden pool, but it didn't impress me: there were no frogs to catch. What's a pond without a polliwog? What did impress me was a painting of a rough-legged hawk tucked among the massive black limbs of an elm tree. I would sit and study this bird as if it were perched to take flight and disappear beyond the painting's borders. I remember the scene as much for the elm tree, since at that time thousands of these stately trees were dying from Dutch elm disease, a deadly fungus spread by the elm bark beetle.

Just beyond the Bateman property was a crazy quilt of fields and concession roads, which I explored with their dog Smallwood, a lumbering and lovable Newfoundland and Labrador cross. Together we hiked Mount Nemo, whose cliffs were a backdrop for circling turkey vultures. In the evenings, I would sit with Bob in his upstairs studio, listening to bird-song recordings and discussing canoeing. Bob would continue painting through our conversations, adding a fly to the nose of an African Cape Buffalo or a fleck of yellow to the savannah.

Bob went on to become one of the world's best-known wildlife artists, but I will always remember those days when he took the time to show me the wonders of the outdoor world. Years later, when I was living in Banff, Bob and his family dropped by while travelling through the Rockies. It was like old times, as we walked the shores of the Vermilion Lakes, our binoculars focused on a nesting osprey. Bob asked me if I thought his children would grow up to share his sense of wonder.

We agreed there were no guarantees, but we also

agreed that parents could guide their children by exposing them to a world beyond concrete and pavement. The children would come to know the feel of soft soil beneath their feet, and they would discover that other adults—not just their parents—are also enthusiastic about the natural world.

Another wonderful mentor I will never forget is Arnold Hodgkins, an artist who shared with me his love of rural tranquility. A spiritual man, Arnold embraced life with a hearty laugh and a twinkling eye. A member of the medical corps during the Second World War, he witnessed life at its cruellest. Upon returning home, he sought peace in the hilly swells near Leaskdale, a small Ontario village that was the home of Lucy Maud Montgomery, creator of Anne of Green Gables. Here Arnold built the Deerfoot Gallery, a unique art space opened in 1963 by A. J. Casson and Frederick Varley of the Group of Seven. Among his paintings were vignettes of leaning barns and lazy country roads vanishing over a round horizon. Left alone in the gallery, I studied these images, imagining what was over each rise and thinking about the animals stabled inside the barns, their heat keeping at bay the cold winter winds.

Arnold's living quarters were dark and subterranean, built beneath his gallery. In his living room was a live tree, its thick bark gnarled and creased with age. It was a part of his home, as familiar and comforting as his old couch and kitchen table. Here was a man who truly lived with nature.

I don't know what I would do without the outdoor world. There is a sense of order in nature that calls to me, whether from a windswept plain, a bluff of aspen, or an aromatic cedar grove. I find a comfort in nature that reminds me of my childhood. On weekends, when we headed to our northern cabin, my homework was done while sitting in the duff beneath a huge white pine. I toyed with mathematics while watching a snapping turtle bask on a half-submerged log. I composed an English essay while canoeing among the lily pads, listening to the mewing and chortling of beaver kittens hidden inside their sticks-and-mud lodge. I contemplated genetics while snowshoeing through waist-high drifts, curious about the bloodied wolverine tracks I was following. So what if I failed sewing class? To me, it never seemed quite as important as knowing how to tap maple trees or how to boil the sap into sweet, sticky syrup.

I wish every child could have the chance to spend time in nature's classroom, guided by gentle wilderness hands. I hope that Jessica and Anne never lose their sense of wonder, and that they pass it on to their own children.

I still see Bob Bateman, usually when he's on a book tour. We still find time to talk about those delightful springs in Ontario when the woods are a carpet of violets and trilliums, about the family of river otters that play outside his home on Salt Spring Island, and about the bears and cougars that wander the aspen trails of my Alberta home. And though Arnold Hodgkins has long since passed away, I am sure he is listening to us. Above our hearth hangs one of his paintings. Entitled *Swamp Cathedral*, it is of a beaver swimming through an arch of bulrushes, its wake forming a large V like flying Canada geese reflected in a sky of water.

Wilderness landscapes remain the bedrock of my life. It was the land that called my mom and me home to Burro Alley. Our lives have moved in a circle, like the earth and its seasons, like day and night, settling in this place that every day massages our souls and rocks us to sleep at night. A place where two ravens view beauty and then take flight to carry its message far and beyond.

About Fifth House

FIFTH HOUSE PUBLISHERS, a Fitzhenry & Whiteside company, is a proudly western-Canadian press. Our publishing specialty is non-fiction as we believe that every community must possess a positive understanding of its worth and place if it is to remain vital and progressive. Fifth House is committed to "bringing the West to the rest" by publishing approximately twenty books a year about the land and people who make this region unique. Our books are selected for their quality, saleability, and contribution to the understanding of western-Canadian (and Canadian) history, culture, and environment.

Look for the following Fifth House titles at your local bookstore:

Bear Tales from the Canadian Rockies,
compiled and edited by Brian Patton, $16.95

Country Calls: Memories of a Small-town Doctor,
Dr. Sid Cornish with Judith Cornish, $14.95

Down on the Farm: Childhood Memories of Farming in Canada,
Jean Cochrane, $12.95

Five Pennies: A Prairie Boy's Story,
Irene Morck, $16.95

The Last Best West: Women on the Alberta Frontier, 1880–1930,
Eliane Leslau Silverman, $14.95

On to the Sunset: The Lifetime Adventures of a Spirited Pioneer,
Ethel Burnett Tibbets, $15.95

(prices subject to change)